Robert Lowry

Select Gems

A choice of collection of popular hymns and music for use in prayer meetings, the home and Sunday schools

Robert Lowry

Select Gems

A choice of collection of popular hymns and music for use in prayer meetings, the home and Sunday schools

ISBN/EAN: 9783337084004

Printed in Europe, USA, Canada, Australia, Japan

Cover: Foto ©Lupo / pixelio.de

More available books at **www.hansebooks.com**

SELECT GEMS

A CHOICE COLLECTION OF

Popular Hymns and Music

FOR USE IN

PRAYER MEETINGS,

THE HOME AND

SUNDAY SCHOOLS.

PHILADELPHIA:
AMERICAN BAPTIST PUBLICATION SOCIETY.
1420 Chestnut St.

Copyright, 1889, by W. H. Doane.

PREFACE.

"Select Gems" is designed for use in the Devotional Meetings of the Church and, also, in the Home Circle and Sunday School. The Hymns have been chosen with a view to secure the best possible expression for the feelings and activities of the Christian Life, and the Music is intended to be inspiring as well as worshipful.

"Select Gems" will be found adapted to every phase of Christian work. It is believed that it will be a great help in times of Revival. Many of the selections, it is hoped, will not only stimulate those who are already Christians, but will attract, and awaken, those who are still unconverted.

No book contains a larger number of pieces endeared, by use, to Christian hearts all over the world; and, besides these, there are many new pieces which in time, we trust, will become equally popular and useful.

Robert Lowry.
W. H. Doane.

March, 1889.

Select Gems

For Devotional Meetings.

"Sing unto the Lord a new song, and his praise in the congregation of saints."—Ps. 149:1.

No. 1.   Praise Ye the Father.

"Thou art my praise."—Jer. 17: 14.

FRIEDRICH F. FLEMMING.

1. Praise ye the Father for His lov-ing kind-ness, Ten-der-ly cares He for His erring children; Praise Him, ye an-gels, praise Him in the heav-ens, Praise ye Je-ho-vah!
2. Praise ye the Sav-iour, great is His com-pas-sion, Gra-ciously cares He for His chosen people; Young men and maid-ens, ye old men and children, Praise ye the Sav-iour!
3. Praise ye the Spir-it, Com-fort-er of Is-rael, Sent of the Fa-ther and the Son to bless us; Praise ye the Fa-ther, Son, and Ho-ly Spir-it, Praise ye the Tri-une God!

No. 2. We Praise Thee, O God.

"I will sing and give praise."—Ps. 108: 1.

Rev. W. P. Mackay.   Rev. John J. Husband.

1. We praise Thee, O God, for the Son of Thy love, For Je-sus who died, and is now gone a-bove.
2. We praise Thee, O God, for Thy Spir-it of light, Who has shown us our Sav-iour, and scattered our night.
3. All glo-ry and praise to the Lamb that was slain, Who has borne all our sins, and has cleansed ev'ry stain.

REFRAIN.

Hal-le-lu-jah! Thine the glo-ry, Hal-le-lu-jah! A-men.
Hal-le-lu-jah! Thine the glo-ry; Re-vive us a-gain.

4 All glory and praise to the God of all grace,
Who has bought us, and sought us, and guided our ways.

5 Revive us again; fill each heart with Thy love;
May each soul be rekindled with fire from above.

No. 3. Holy, Holy, Lord.

"They rest not day and night, saying, Holy, holy, holy, Lord God Almighty."—Rev. 4: 8.

Reginald Heber, D. D.   Rev. J. B. Dykes.

1. Ho-ly, ho-ly, ho-ly, Lord God Al-might-y! Gladly with de-
2. Ho-ly, ho-ly, ho-ly, all the saints a-dore Thee, Casting down their
3. Ho-ly, ho-ly, ho-ly, Lord God Al-might-y! All Thy works shall

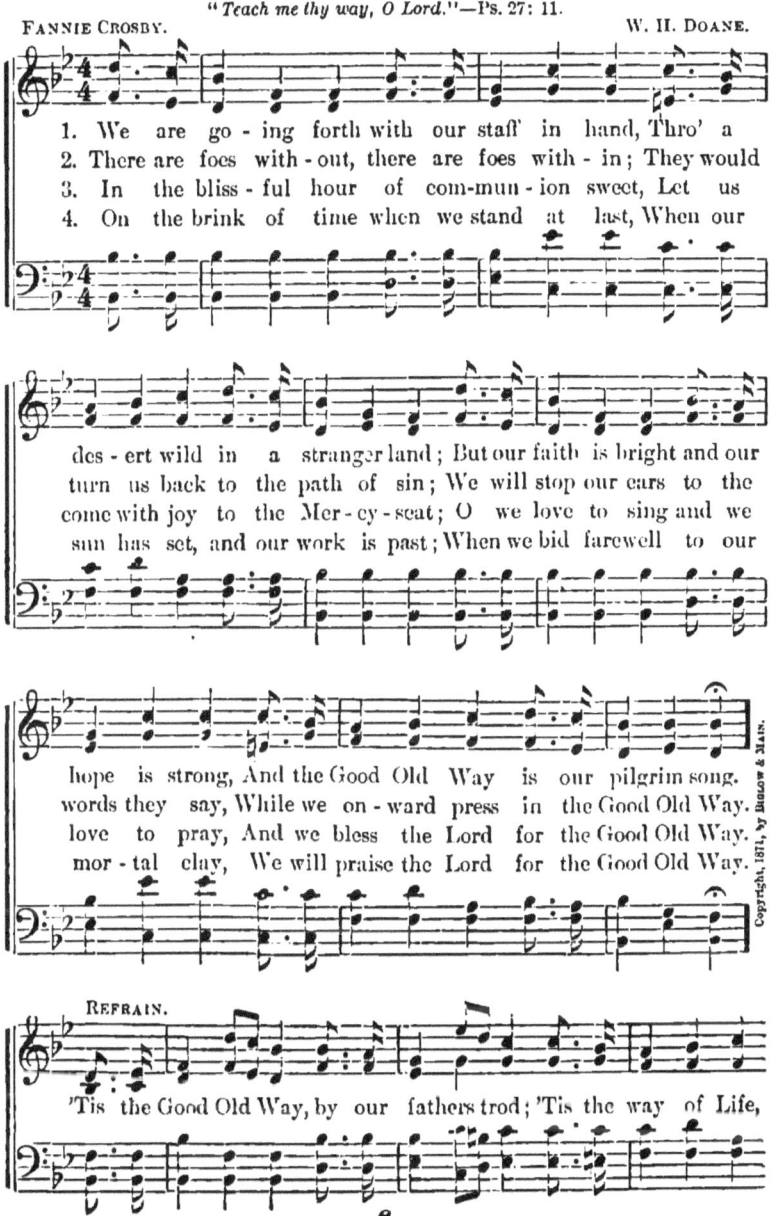

The Good Old Way. Concluded.

And it lead-eth un-to God; 'Tis the on-ly path to the realms of day; We are go-ing home in the Good Old Way.

No. 6. Saviour, to Thy Mercy Seat.

"*Draw near with a true heart.*"—HEB. 10: 22.

WM. STEVENSON.   ROBERT LOWRY.

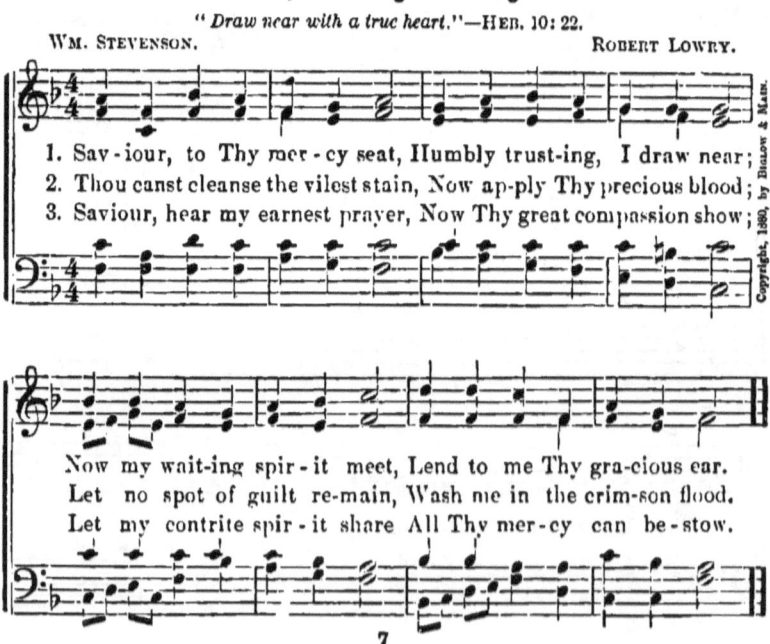

1. Sav-iour, to Thy mer-cy seat, Humbly trust-ing, I draw near; Now my wait-ing spir-it meet, Lend to me Thy gra-cious ear.
2. Thou canst cleanse the vilest stain, Now ap-ply Thy precious blood; Let no spot of guilt re-main, Wash me in the crim-son flood.
3. Saviour, hear my earnest prayer, Now Thy great compassion show; Let my contrite spir-it share All Thy mer-cy can be-stow.

No. 8. I Love to Tell the Story.

"I will tell thee."—Num. 23: 3.

KATE HANKEY.   WM. G. FISCHER, by per.

1. I love to tell the story Of un-seen things a-bove, Of Je-sus and His glo-ry, Of Je-sus and His love. I love to tell the story, Because I know it's true; It sat-is-fies my longings As nothing else can do.

2. I love to tell the story; More wonder-ful it seems Than all the golden fancies Of all our golden dreams. I love to tell the story, It did so much for me! And that is just the rea-son I tell it now to thee.

3. I love to tell the story; 'Tis pleasant to re-peat What seems, each time I tell it, More wonderful-ly sweet. I love to tell the story, For some have never heard The message of sal-va-tion From God's own holy word.

4. I love to tell the story; For those who know it best Seem hun-ger-ing and thirsting To hear it like the rest. And when in scenes of glo-ry I sing the New, New Song, 'Twill be the Old, Old Story That I have loved so long.

REFRAIN.

I love to tell the sto-ry, 'Twill be my theme in glo-ry, To tell the old, old sto-ry Of Je-sus and His love.

No. 16. Gather Them In.

"Go out into the highways and hedges, and compel them to come in." —LUKE 14: 23.

FANNY J. CROSBY.   GEO. C. STEBBINS.

Copyright, 1883, by Geo. C. Stebbins.

1. Gath-er them in, for there yet is room At the feast that a King has spread; O gath-er them in, let His house be filled, And the hun-gry and poor be fed.

2. Gath-er them in, for there yet is room; But our hearts, how they throb with pain, To think of the ma-ny who slight the call That may nev-er be heard a-gain.

3. Gath-er them in, for there yet is room; 'Tis a mes-sage from God a-bove; O gath-er them in-to the fold of grace, And the arms of the Sav-iour's love.

REFRAIN.

Out in the high-way, out in the by-way, Out in the dark depths of sin, Go forth, go forth with a lov-ing heart, And gather the wand'rers in.

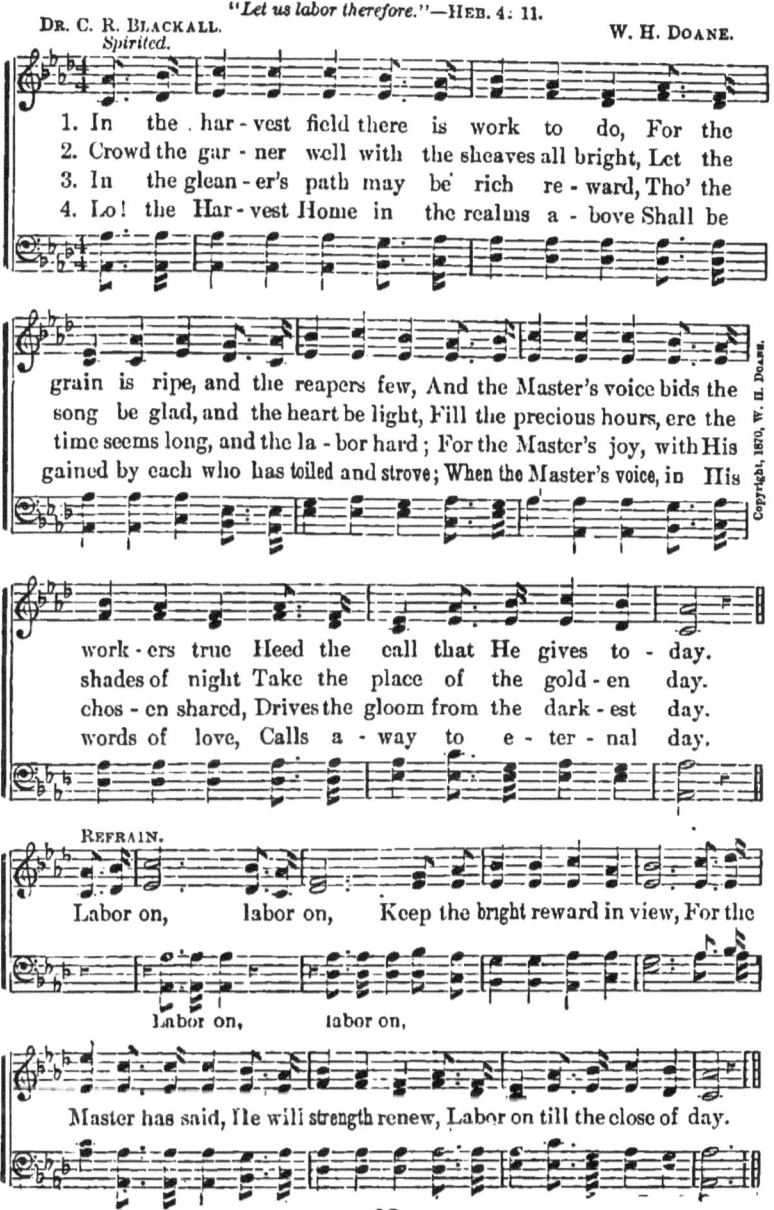

No. 19. To the Work.

"Work, for I am with you."—HAG. 2: 4.

FANNY J. CROSBY.   W. H. DOANE.

Copyright, 1871, Biglow & Main.

1. To the work! to the work! we are serv-ants of God, Let us fol-low the path that our Mas-ter has trod; With the balm of his coun-sel our strength to re-new, Let us do with our might what our hands find to do. Toil-ing on, Toil-ing on, Toil-ing on, Toil-ing on, Let us Toil-ing on, Toil-ing on, Toil-ing on,

2. To the work! to the work! let the hun-gry be fed; To the fount-ain of Life let the wea-ry be led; In the cross and its ban-ner our glo-ry shall be, While we her-ald the ti-dings, "Sal-va-tion is free!"

3. To the work! to the work! there is la-bor for all, For the king-dom of dark-ness and er-ror shall fall; And the name of Je-ho-vah ex-alt-ed shall be In the loud swelling cho-rus, "Sal-va-tion is free!"

To the Work. Concluded.

hope, Let us watch, And la-bor till the Mas-ter comes.
and trust, and pray,

No. 20. Work, for the Night.

"The night cometh."—JOHN 9: 4.

ANNA L. WALKER.   DR. LOWELL MASON, by per.

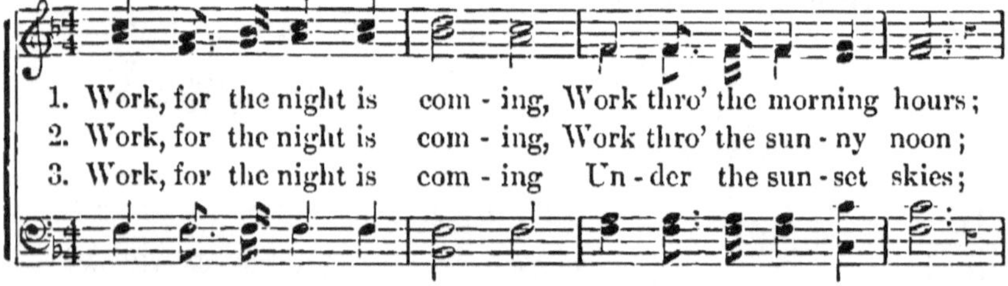

1. Work, for the night is com-ing, Work thro' the morning hours;
2. Work, for the night is com-ing, Work thro' the sun-ny noon;
3. Work, for the night is com-ing Un-der the sun-set skies;

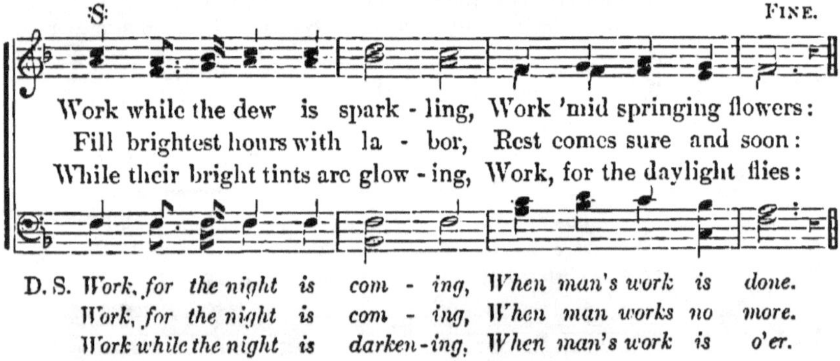

Work while the dew is spark-ling, Work 'mid springing flowers:
Fill brightest hours with la-bor, Rest comes sure and soon:
While their bright tints are glow-ing, Work, for the daylight flies:

D. S. Work, for the night is com-ing, When man's work is done.
  Work, for the night is com-ing, When man works no more.
  Work while the night is darken-ing, When man's work is o'er.

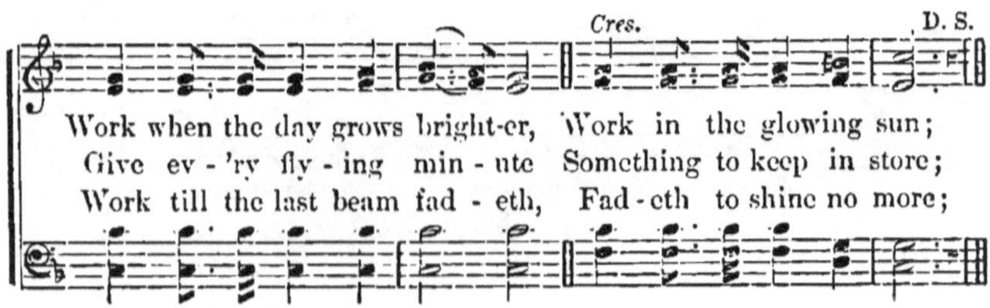

Work when the day grows bright-er, Work in the glowing sun;
Give ev-'ry fly-ing min-ute Something to keep in store;
Work till the last beam fad-eth, Fad-eth to shine no more;

I was Glad. Concluded.

I was glad, To be fed on His life-giving word.
I was glad,

No. 22. Sweet Moments of Prayer.

"There I will meet with thee, and I will commune."—EXOD. 25: 22.

FANNIE J. CROSBY. W. H. DOANE. 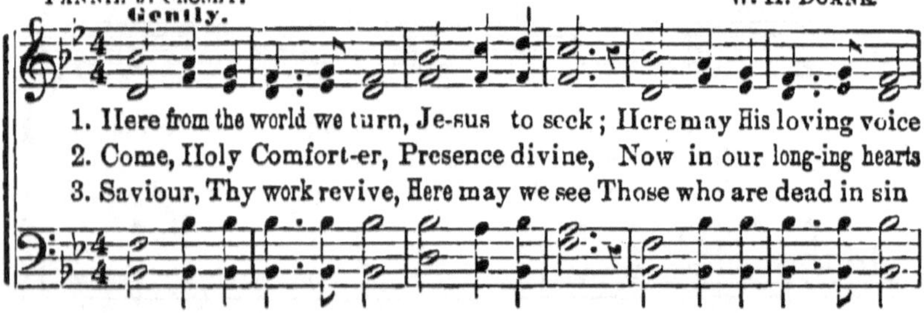
Gently.

1. Here from the world we turn, Jesus to seek; Here may His loving voice Tenderly speak; Jesus, our dearest friend, While at Thy feet we bend, O let Thy smile descend, 'Tis Thee we seek.
2. Come, Holy Comfort-er, Presence divine, Now in our longing hearts Graciously shine; O for Thy mighty Power, O for a blessed show'r Filling this hallowed hour With joy divine.
3. Saviour, Thy work revive, Here may we see Those who are dead in sin Quickened by Thee; Come to our hearts to-night, Make ev'ry burden light, Cheer thou our waiting sight, We long for Thee.

Copyright, 1874, by W. H. Doane.

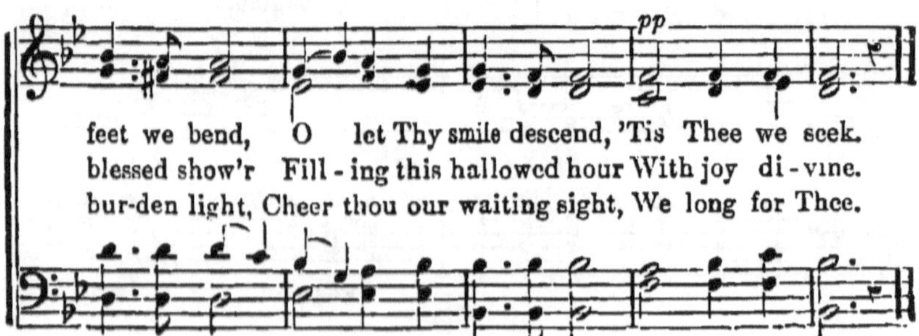

O, the Blessed Cross! Concluded.

I will cling, ... Till my Saviour's crown of life I wear.

To the blessed cross I'll cling,

No. 26. Loving Kindness.

"How excellent is thy loving kindness."—Ps. 36: 7.

REV. SAMUEL MEDLEY.   OLD MELODY.

1. A-wake, my soul, in joy-ful lays, And sing Thy great Redeemer's praise;
2. He saw me ru-ined by the fall, Yet loved me, notwithstanding all;
3. I oft-en feel my sinful heart Prone from my Saviour to de-part;
4. Soon shall I pass the gloomy vale, Soon all my mortal powers must fail;

He just-ly claims a song from me, His loving kindness, O, how free!
He saved me from my lost estate, His loving kindness, O, how great!
But though I oft have Him forgot, His loving kindness changes not.
O, may my last, expiring breath, His loving kindness sing in death.

REFRAIN.

His loving kindness, loving kindness, His loving kindness, O, how free!

No. 27. The Lord is My Light.

"The Lord is my light and my salvation."—Ps. 27: 1.

JAMES NICHOLSON.   J. W. BISCHOFF, by per.

1. The Lord is my light, then why should I fear? By day and by night
2. The Lord is my light, tho' clouds may arise; Faith stronger than sight
3. The Lord is my light, the Lord is my strength; I know in His might

His pres-ence is near; He is my sal-va-tion from sorrow and sin;
looks up to the skies, Where Jesus for-ev - er in glo-ry doth reign;
I'll conquer at length; My weakness in mercy He covers with pow'r,

D. S. *The Lord is my light, my joy and my song;*

This bless-ed per-sua-sion the Spir-it brings in.
Oh! how can I ev - er in darkness remain? The Lord is my
And walking by faith He saves me each hour.

By day and by night He leads me a-long.

light, my joy and my song; By day and by night He leads me along;

No. 30. Blessed Hour of Prayer.

"—went up together into the temple at the hour of prayer."—ACTS. 3: 1.

FANNY J. CROSBY.   W. H. DOANE.

1. 'Tis the blessed hour of prayer, when our hearts low-ly bend, And we
2. 'Tis the blessed hour of prayer, when the Saviour draws near, With a
3. 'Tis the blessed hour of prayer, when the tempted and tried To the
4. At the blessed hour of prayer, trusting Him, we be-lieve That the

gather to Jesus, our Saviour and Friend; If we come to Him in
tender compassion His children to hear; When He tells us we may
Saviour who loves them their sorrow confide; With a sym-pa-thiz-ing
blessing we're needing we'll sure-ly re-ceive; In the fullness of this

faith, His pro-tection to share, What a balm for the weary! O how
cast at His feet ev-'ry care, What a balm for the weary! O how
heart He removes ev-'ry care; What a balm for the weary! O how
trust we shall lose ev'ry care; What a balm for the weary! O how

D. S. *What a balm for the weary! O how*

FINE. REFRAIN.   D. S.

sweet to be there! Blessed hour of pray'r, Blessed hour of pray'r;

sweet to be there!

Copyright, 1891, by Fillmore & Main.

Freely it Flows. Concluded.

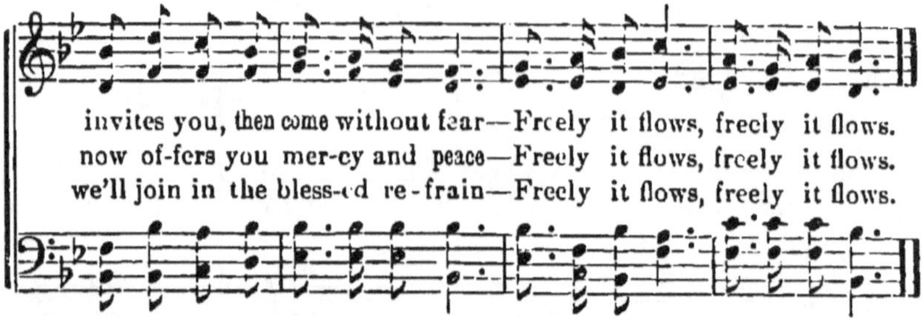

invites you, then come without fear—Freely it flows, freely it flows.
now of-fers you mer-cy and peace—Freely it flows, freely it flows.
we'll join in the bless-ed re-frain—Freely it flows, freely it flows.

No. 32.   Rest in Jesus.

"Come unto me, ... and I will give you rest."—MATT. 11: 28.

FANNY J. CROSBY.   W. H. DOANE.

1. Come with all Thy sor-row, Wea-ry, wandering soul!
2. He, thy strength in weak-ness, Will thy ref-uge be;
3. Come in faith, be-liev-ing, To His will re-signed;
4. See the door of mer-cy! Wouldst thou enter there?

REFRAIN.

Come to Him who loves thee—He will make thee whole.
Cast on Him thy bur-den— He will care for thee.   There is rest in
Ask, and He will give thee; Seek, and thou shalt find.
Knock, and He will o-pen; Lo! the key is prayer.

p   Rit.

Je-sus, sweet, sweet rest: There is rest in Je-sus, sweet, sweet rest.

No. 34. My Soul will Overcome.

"They overcame him by the blood of the Lamb."—Rev. 12: 11.

R. L.
Robert Lowry.

Copyright, 1877, by R. Lowry.

1. Helpless I come to Jesus' blood, And all myself resign;
I lose my weakness in that flood, And gather strength divine.

2. 'Tis Jesus gives me life within, And nerves me for the fray;
He spoiled the hosts of death and sin, And took their pow'r away.

3. Tho' clouds of conflict hide my view, And foes are fierce and strong,
In Jesus' name I'll struggle thro', And enter heav'n with song.

REFRAIN.

My soul will overcome by the blood of the Lamb, My soul will overcome by the blood of the Lamb; Overcome, overcome, Overcome by the blood of the Lamb.

No. 35. Be Near Me, Saviour.

"Call ye upon him while he is near."—ISA. 55: 6.

EL NATHAN.   H. H. McGRANAHAN.

1. Be near me, O my Sav-iour, For this a-lone I pray; Thy Spir-it free, O give to me, While here on earth I stay.
2. Be near me, O my Sav-iour, By morn, by noon, by night; Thus constant keep Thy wand'ring sheep, In paths of truth and right.
3. Be near me when tempta-tions My soul, so weak, as-sail; As then I cry to Thee on high, Let not Thy promise fail.
4. Be near me when to Jor-dan My wea-ry feet draw nigh, My faith sus-tain thro' all my pain, And give me grace to die.

REFRAIN.

Be near me, O be near me, Thou Lamb of Cal-va-ry; Dwell in my heart and grace impart, To live and die for Thee.

Copyright, 1886, by H. H. McGranahan.

No. 36. Keep Praying as You Go.

"Pray without ceasing."—1 Thess. 5: 17.

C. J. F.   W. H. Doane.

1. Come, burdened souls, with all your guilt, And all your weight of woe,
2. Be-hold the precious Lamb who died For man, His love to show;
3. Now, soldiers, gird your ar-mor on, And bold-ly meet the foe;
4. Ye pilgrims on the heav'n-ly way, Thro' trials here be-low,

There's mer-cy at a Throne of grace; Keep praying as you go.
And while you seek the blood-stained cross, Keep praying as you go.
Let faith di-rect, and hope in-spire; Keep praying as you go.
O, nev-er doubt a Saviour's love; Keep praying as you go.

REFRAIN.

Keep pray-ing, ev-er pray-ing, Thro' all your journey be-low; To Je-sus, to Je-sus, Keep praying as you go.

Copyright, 1871, by Biglow & Main.

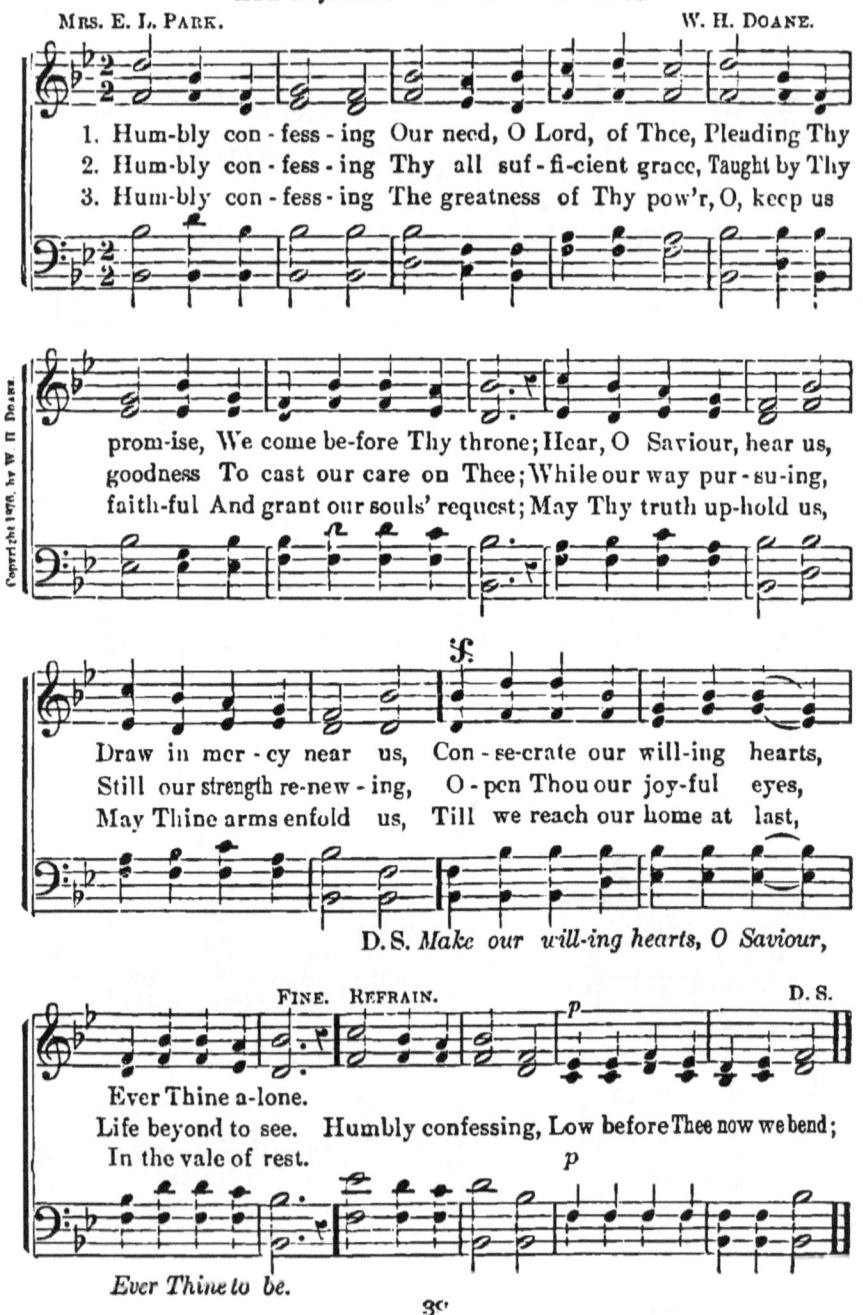

No. 39. Come with Thy Broken Heart.

"The Lord is nigh unto them that are of a broken heart." —Ps. 31:18.

FANNY J. CROSBY.   T. E. PERKINS.

1. Come, oh, come with thy broken heart, La-den with sin and care;
2. Firm-ly cling to the bless-ed cross, There shall thy refuge be;
3. Come and taste of the precious feast, Feast of e-ter-nal love;

D. C. *Come, oh, come with thy broken heart, Wea-ry and worn with care;*

Come and kneel at the o-pen door, Je-sus is wait-ing there;
Wash thee now in the crim-son fount, Flowing so pure for thee;
Think of joys that for ev-er bloom, Bright in the life a-bove;

Come and kneel at the o-pen door, Je-sus is wait-ing there.

Wait-ing to heal thy wounded soul, Waiting to give thee rest;
List to the gen-tle warn-ing voice, List to the ear-nest call;
Come with a trusting heart to God, Come and be saved by grace;

D. C. *for Refrain.*

Why wilt thou walk where shadows fall? Come to His lov-ing breast.
Leave at the cross thy bur-den now, Je-sus will bear it all.
Come, for He loves to clasp thee now, Close in His dear em-brace.

No. 42. Jesus will Help You.

"Grace to help in time of need."—HEB. 4: 16.

WM. STEVENSON. ROBERT LOWRY.

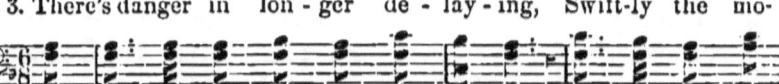

1. The Sav-iour is call-ing you, sin-ner—Urg-ing you now
2. Thro' Him there is life in be-liev-ing; Sin-ner, O why
3. There's danger in lon-ger de-lay-ing, Swift-ly the mo-

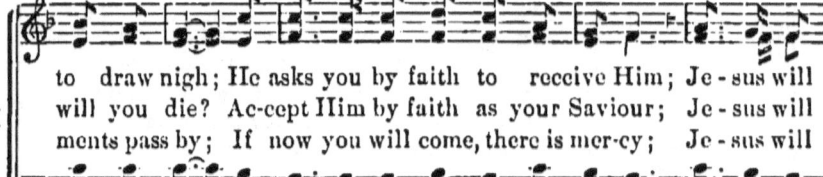

to draw nigh; He asks you by faith to receive Him; Je-sus will
will you die? Ac-cept Him by faith as your Saviour; Je-sus will
ments pass by; If now you will come, there is mer-cy; Je-sus will

help if you try.
help if you try. Je-sus will help you, Je-sus will help you,
help if you try.

Help you with grace from on high; The weak-est and poor-est the

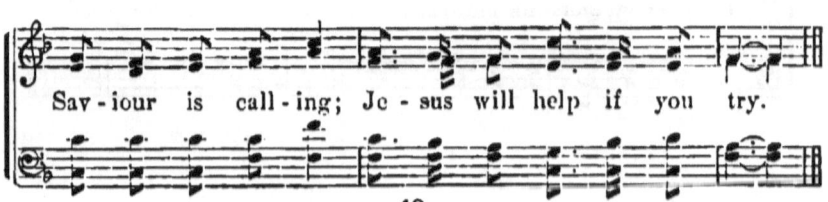

Sav-iour is call-ing; Je-sus will help if you try.

No. 43. Follow On.

"If any man serve me, let him follow me."—JOHN 12: 26.

W. O. CUSHING. ROBERT LOWRY.

1. Down in the val-ley with my Sav-iour I would go,
2. Down in the val-ley with my Sav-iour I would go,
3. Down in the val-ley, or up-on the mountain steep,

Where the flow'rs are bloom-ing and the sweet wa-ters flow;
Where the storms are sweep-ing and the dark wa-ters flow:
Close be-side my Sav-iour would my soul ev-er keep;

Ev-'ry-where He leads me I would fol-low, fol-low on,
With His hand to lead me I will nev-er, nev-er fear;
He will lead me safe-ly in the path that He has trod,

Walk-ing in His foot-steps till the crown be won.
Dan-gers can-not fright me if my Lord is near.
Up to where they gath-er on the hills of God.

Copyright, 1880, by Biglow & Main.

REFRAIN.

Fol-low, fol-low, I would fol-low Je-sus, A-ny-where,

Follow On. Concluded.

ev-'rywhere, I would fol-low on; Fol-low, fol-low, I would fol-low Je-sus, Ev'rywhere He leads me, I would fol-low on.

No. 44.   More, more like Thee.

"We shall be like him."—1 John 3: 2.

Mrs. Edna L. Park.   W. H. Doane.

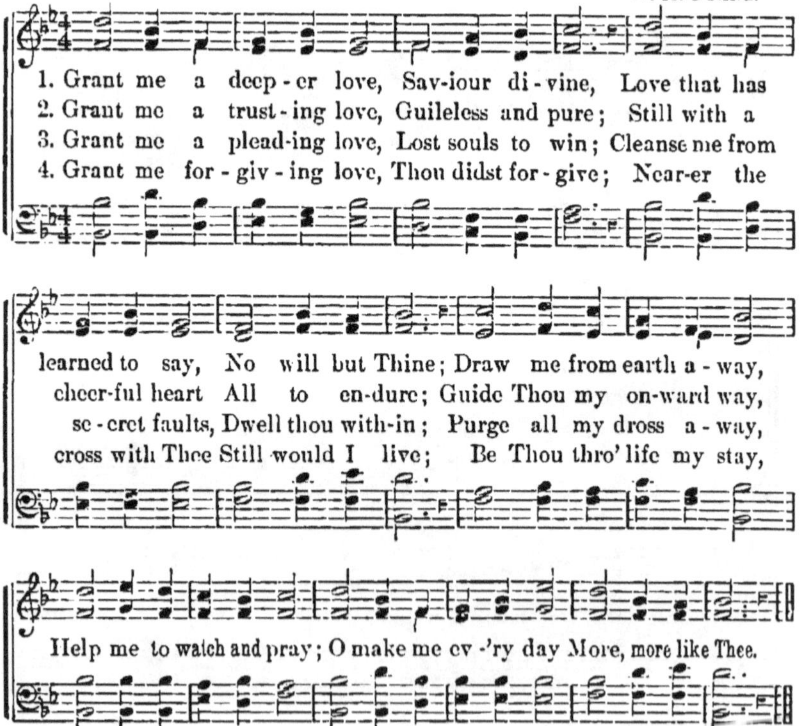

1. Grant me a deep-er love, Sav-iour di-vine, Love that has learned to say, No will but Thine; Draw me from earth a-way,
2. Grant me a trust-ing love, Guileless and pure; Still with a cheer-ful heart All to en-dure; Guide Thou my on-ward way,
3. Grant me a plead-ing love, Lost souls to win; Cleanse me from se-cret faults, Dwell thou with-in; Purge all my dross a-way,
4. Grant me for-giv-ing love, Thou didst for-give; Near-er the cross with Thee Still would I live; Be Thou thro' life my stay,

Help me to watch and pray; O make me ev-'ry day More, more like Thee.

Copyright, 1864, by Biglow & Main.

45

No. 45. I could not do without Thee.

"*I will never leave thee, nor forsake thee.*"—HEB. 13: 5.

FRANCES RIDLEY HAVERGAL.   ROBERT LOWRY.

1. I could not do with-out Thee, O Sav-iour of the lost,
2. I could not do with-out Thee, For O, the way is long;
3. I could not do with-out Thee, For years are fleet-ing fast,

Whose precious blood redeemed me At such tremendous cost;
And I am oft-en wea-ry, And sigh re-plac-es song;
And now in sol-emn si-lence The riv-er must be passed;

Thy righteousness, Thy par-don, Thy sac-ri-fice, must be
How could I do with-out Thee? I do not know the way;
But Thou wilt nev-er leave me, And, tho' the waves roll high,

My on-ly hope and com-fort, My glo-ry and my plea.
Thou knowest, and Thou lead-est, And wilt not let me stray.
I know Thou wilt be near me, And whisper, "It is I."

No. 49. What is all the world to Me?

"Lo! I am with you alway." —MATT. 28: 20.

R. L.
ROBERT LOWRY.

1. What is all the world to me, With my Saviour near me?
2. How can sense be-guile my soul, When my Saviour loves me?
3. Why should du-ty dark ap-pear, If my Saviour sends me?
4. All my way I trust to Him, Je-sus now re-ceives me;

What is all the mirth I see, With my Lord to cheer me?
How can sin my heart con-trol, When my Lord approves me?
Why should dan-ger give me fear, If my Lord befriends me?
All my way till sight grows dim, Je-sus nev-er leaves me.

REFRAIN.

"Lo! I am with you al-way, Lo! I am with you alway;"

O pre-cious is that word! Prom-ise sweet of Je-sus.

Copyright, 1880, by Biglow & Main.

No. 51. Lowly at Thy Feet.

"He giveth grace unto the lowly."—Prov. 3: 34.

FANNY J. CROSBY.   W. H. DOANE.

Tenderly.

1. Low-ly at Thy feet, O Saviour, I am kneel-ing, Breathing a pray'r of pen-i-tence to Thee; Whither can I go? Thou art my on-ly refuge; Lord, I have sinned, but Thou hast died for me.
2. Low-ly at Thy feet, O Saviour, I am kneel-ing, Helpless I come, for Thou hast said I may; 'Tis Thy promised word my broken heart is pleading; Thou wilt not turn the pen-i-tent a-way.
3. Low-ly at Thy feet, O Saviour, I am kneel-ing, Thy precious blood will cleanse from ev'ry sin; O-pen Thou mine eyes that I may see the fountain: Wash me, O Lord, and make me pure within.
4. Low-ly at Thy feet, O Saviour, I am kneel-ing, Thy voice a-lone can bid my spir-it live; Take me as I am, my faith to Thee is clinging; Now, blessed Lord, the pen-i-tent for-give.

REFRAIN.

Low-ly, low-ly at Thy feet I fall, Saviour, Saviour, hear, O hear my call.

Copyright, 1887, by W. H. Doane.

No. 52. I'm Kneeling at the Door.

"Knock, and it shall be opened unto you." — Matt. 7: 7.

Mrs. Lydia C. Baxter.   T. E. Perkins.

Copyright, 1878, by T. E. Perkins.

1. I'm kneeling, Lord, at mercy's gate, With trembling hope and fear;
2. None ev-er emp-ty turned a-way, Who tru-ly sought Thy face;
3. And when the ransomed millions stand On Zi-on's flow'r-y hill,

I've wait-ed long, and still I wait: Thy gracious voice to hear;
And I, my Sav-iour, come to-day, To seek Thy pardoning grace;
With palms of vic-t'ry in their hand, Waiting their Master's will

Thy precious word has bid me seek The joys Thou hast in store;
Thy precious blood is all my plea; This can my soul re-store;
Oh, may I bear the liv-ing green, And that dear name a-dore,

FINE.

O Lord, in mer-cy speak to me, I'm kneeling at the door.
O Lord, in mer-cy speak to me, I'm kneeling at the door.
Whose love the sin-ner did re-deem, While kneeling at the door.

REFRAIN.   D. S.

I'm kneel-ing at the door, Kneel-ing at the door;
I'm kneel-ing at the door, Kneel-ing at the door;
While kneel-ing at the door, Kneel-ing at the door;

No. 53. Love of Jesus.

"Thy love and faith, which thou hast toward the Lord Jesus."—PHILEM. 1: 5.

W. O. CUSHING.   ROBERT LOWRY.

1. Let my heart be pure from sin, Filled with the love of Je-sus;
2. To my lips Thy truth impart, Filled with the love of Je-sus;
3. O what joy my soul hath known, Filled with the love of Je-sus;

Help me, Lord, Thy grace to win, Filled with the love of Je-sus;
Be my wayward, restless heart, Filled with the love of Je-sus;
Trusting still Thy grace a-lone, Filled with the love of Je-sus;

All Thou bid'st me I would do, While Thy lov-ing life I view;
All I do, or think, or say, All my life from day to day,
Come, ye souls in bondage sore, Come and here His grace implore;

Faithful be my heart and true, Filled with the love of Je-sus.
All be Thine, O Lord, I pray, Filled with the love of Je-sus.
Ye shall taste and thirst no more, Filled with the love of Je-sus.

Copyright, 1884, by Biglow & Main.

No. 59. Whisper a Message.

"A message from God unto thee."—JUDGES 3: 20.

MYRA JUDSON.   W. H. DOANE.

1. Saviour, the day is de-clin-ing, O for a moment with
2. All the day long I have la-bored, Now would I tar-ry with
3. Soft as the zeph-yr that murmured Ten-der-ly o-ver the
4. Un-der Thy ban-ner of mer-cy, Guarded and safe would I

Thee; Come in the hush of the twi-light, Whis-per a
Thee; Come, for I need Thy re-fresh-ing, Whis-per a
sea, Come at this hour of de-vo-tion, Whis-per a
be; Je-sus, my Bless-ed Re-deem-er, Whis-per a

Copyright 1883, by W. H. Doane.

REFRAIN. *pp*

mes-sage to me. Whis-per, whis-per, Soft-ly whis-per Thy

pp

love in my heart; Whisper, whisper, Whisper Thy love in my heart.

No. 61. Jesus! Lover of My Soul.

"Thou art my refuge."—Ps. 142: 5.

REV. CHARLES WESLEY.　　　　　　　　　　　　　SIMEON B. MARSH.

1. Je-sus! lov-er of my soul, Let me to Thy bo-som fly,
   While the rag-ing billows roll, While the tem-pest still is high.
   D.C. Safe in-to the ha-ven guide, Oh, re-ceive my soul at last.

Hide me, O my Sav-iour! hide, Till the storm of life is past;

2 Other refuge have I none;
　Hangs my helpless soul on Thee;
Leave, ah! leave me not alone,
　Still support and comfort me.
All my trust on Thee is stayed;
　All my help from Thee I bring;
Cover my defenseless head
　With the shadow of Thy wing.

3 Thou, O Christ, art all I want;
　All in all in Thee I find;
Raise the fallen, cheer the faint,
　Heal the sick, and lead the blind.
Just and holy is Thy name,
　I am all unrighteousness;
Vile and full of sin I am,
　Thou art full of truth and grace.

No. 62. Rock of Ages.

"The Rock of my refuge."—Ps. 94: 22.

REV. A. M. TOPLADY.　　　　　　　　　　　　DR. THOS. HASTINGS.

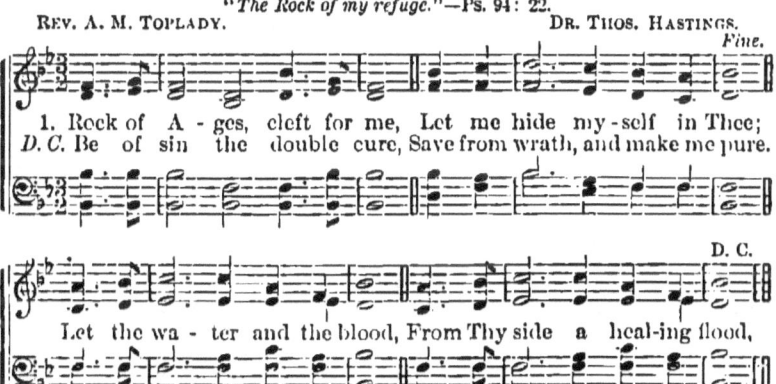

1. Rock of A-ges, cleft for me, Let me hide my-self in Thee;
   D.C. Be of sin the double cure, Save from wrath, and make me pure.

Let the wa-ter and the blood, From Thy side a heal-ing flood,

2 Should my tears forever flow,
　Should my zeal no languor know,
All for sin could not atone;
Thou must save, and Thou alone;
　In my hand no price I bring;
Simply to Thy cross I cling.

3 While I draw this fleeting breath,
　When mine eyelids close in death,
When I rise to worlds unknown,
See Thee on Thy judgment throne—
　Rock of Ages, cleft for me,
Let me hide myself in Thee.

No. 63. Nearer, My God.

"Draw near with a true heart."—HEB. 10: 22.

SARAH F. ADAMS.   DR. LOWELL MASON, by per.

2 Though like the wanderer,
  The sun gone down,
Darkness comes over me,
  My rest a stone,
Yet in my dreams I'd be
Nearer, my God, to Thee,
  Nearer to Thee!

3 There let my way appear
  Steps unto heaven;
All that Thou sendest me
  In mercy given;

Angels to beckon me
Nearer, my God, to Thee,
  Nearer to Thee!

4 Then with my waking thoughts
  Bright with Thy praise,
Out of my stony griefs
  Bethel I'll raise;
So by my woes to be
Nearer, my God, to Thee,
  Nearer to Thee!

No. 64. Must Jesus Bear the Cross.

"Endured the cross."—HEB. 12: 2.

THOS. SHEPHERD.   GEORGE N. ALLEN.

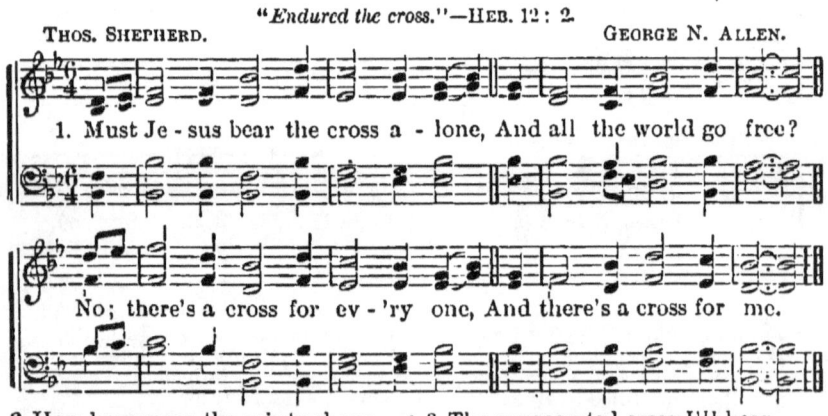

2 How happy are the saints above,
  Who once went sorrowing here;
But now they taste unmingled love,
  And joy without a tear.

3 The consecrated cross I'll bear
  Till death shall set me free,
And then go home my crown to wear,
  For there's a crown for me.

No. 65. My Faith Looks Up.

"Stand fast in the faith."—1 Cor. 16: 13.

DR. RAY PALMER.   DR. LOWELL MASON.

1. My faith looks up to Thee, Thou Lamb of Calvary, Sav-iour divine;

{ Now hear me while I pray; }
{ Take all my guilt a-way; } O let me from this day Be wholly Thine.

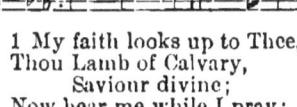

1 My faith looks up to Thee,
Thou Lamb of Calvary,
  Saviour divine;
Now hear me while I pray;
Take all my guilt away;
O let me from this day
  Be wholly Thine.

2 May Thy rich grace impart
Strength to my fainting heart—
  My zeal inspire;
As Thou hast died for me,
O, may my love to Thee,
Pure, warm, and changeless be—
  A living fire.

3 While life's dark maze I tread,
And griefs around me spread,
  Be Thou my Guide;
Bid darkness turn to day,
Wipe sorrow's tears away,
Nor let me ever stray
  From Thee aside.

4 When ends life's transient dream,
When death's cold, sullen stream
  Shall o'er me roll;
Blest Saviour, then, in love,
Fear and distress remove;
Oh, bear me safe above,
  A ransomed soul!

No. 66. I am Trusting, Lord.

"In thee is my trust."—Ps. 141: 8.

W. H. McDONALD.   WM. G. FISCHER, by per.

Ref.—I am trusting, Lord, in Thee, O Thou Lamb of Calvary; Humbly at Thy cross I bow, Save me, Jesus, save me now.

1 I am coming to the cross;
  I am poor, and weak, and blind;
I am counting all but dross;
  I shall full salvation find.

2 Here I give my all to Thee,—
  Friends, and time, and earthly store;
Soul and body Thine to be—
  Wholly Thine—for evermore.

3 In the promises I trust;
  Now I feel the blood applied;
I am prostrate in the dust;
  I with Christ am crucified.

4 Jesus comes! He fills my soul!
  Perfected in love I am;
I am every whit made whole;
  Glory, glory to the Lamb!

No. 67. Something for Jesus.

"With faith and love." —1 Tim. 1: 14.

S. D. Phelps, D. D. Robert Lowry.

1. { Saviour, Thy dying love Thou gavest me,
     Nor should I aught withhold, Dear (*Omit*) .. } Lord, from Thee; In love my soul would bow, My heart fulfill its vow, Some offering bring Thee now, Something for Thee.

2 O'er the blest mercy-seat,
  Pleading for me,
Upward in faith I look,
  Jesus, to Thee;
Help me the cross to bear,
Thy wondrous love declare,
Some song to raise, or prayer,
  Something for Thee.

3 Give me a faithful heart,
  Likeness to Thee—
That each departing day
  Henceforth may see
Some work of love begun,
Some deed of kindness done,
Some wanderer sought and won,
  Something for Thee.

4 All that I am and have—
  Thy gifts so free—
Ever, in joy or grief,
  My Lord, for Thee!
And when Thy face I see,
My ransomed soul shall be,
Through all eternity,
  Something for Thee.

No. 68. Naomi.

"He giveth grace unto the lowly." —Prov. 3: 31.

Anne Steele. Dr. Lowell Mason.

1. Father, whate'er of earthly bliss Thy sovereign will denies, Accepted at Thy throne of grace, Let this petition rise:

2 Give me a calm, a thankful heart,
  From every murmur free;
The blessings of Thy grace impart,
  And make me live to Thee.

3 Let the sweet hope that Thou art mine,
  My life and death attend;
Thy presence thro' my journey shine,
  And crown my journey's end.

No. 69. Bless Me Now.

"I will bless thee."—HEB. 6: 14.

REV. ALEXANDER CLARK. ROBERT LOWRY.

1. Heavenly Father, bless me now; At the cross of Christ I bow; Take my guilt and grief away;

REFRAIN.
Hear and heal me now, I pray. Bless me now, Bless me now, Heavenly Father, bless me now.

Copyright, 1873, by Biglow & Main.

2 Now, O Lord, this very hour,
Send Thy grace and show Thy power;
While I rest upon Thy word,
Come and bless me now, O Lord!

3 Now, just now, for Jesus' sake,
Lift the clouds, the fetters break;
While I look, and as I cry,
Touch and cleanse me ere I die.

4 Never did I so adore
Jesus Christ, Thy Son, before;
Now the time! and this the place!
Gracious Father, show Thy grace.

No. 70. Nettleton.

"Give me a blessing."—JUDGES 1: 15.

REV. R. ROBINSON. JOHN WYETH. *Fine.*

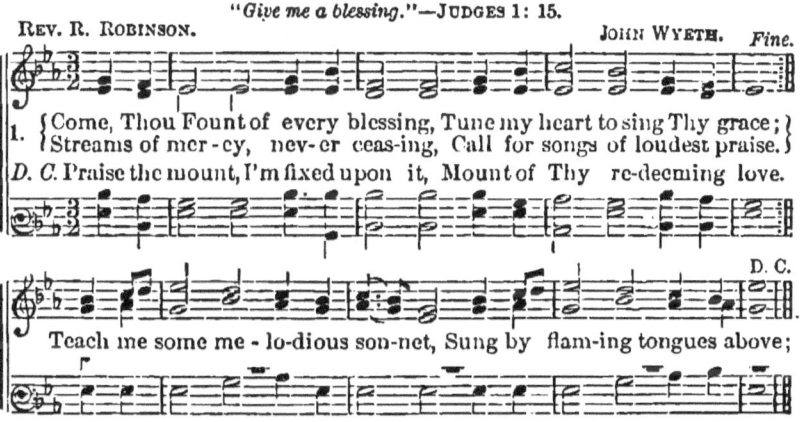

1. { Come, Thou Fount of every blessing, Tune my heart to sing Thy grace; }
   { Streams of mer-cy, nev-er ceas-ing, Call for songs of loudest praise. }
D. C. Praise the mount, I'm fixed upon it, Mount of Thy re-deeming love.

Teach me some me-lo-dious son-net, Sung by flam-ing tongues above;

2 Here I raise my Ebenezer;
Hither by Thy help I'm come;
And I hope, by Thy good pleasure,
Safely to arrive at home;
Jesus sought me when a stranger,
Wandering from the fold of God;
He, to rescue me from danger,
Interposed His precious blood.

3 O, to grace how great a debtor
Daily I'm constrained to be!
Let Thy goodness, like a fetter,
Bind my wandering heart to Thee;
Prone to wander, Lord, I feel it;
Prone to leave the God I love;
Here's my heart, O, take and seal it;
Seal it from Thy courts above.

No. 72. Sweet Hour of Prayer.

"At the hour of prayer."—ACTS. 3 : 1.

REV. WM. W. WALFORD. WM. B. BRADBURY.

1. Sweet hour of prayer, sweet hour of prayer, That calls me from a world of care,
And bids me, at my Father's throne, Make all my wants and (*Omit.*) wishes known!
D. C. And oft escaped the tempter's snare, By thy return, sweet (*Omit.*) hour of prayer.

In sea-sons of distress and grief, My soul has oft - en found relief,

2 Sweet hour of prayer, sweet hour of prayer,
Thy wings shall my petition bear
To Him, whose truth and faithfulness
Engage the waiting soul to bless:
And since He bids me seek His face,
Believe His word, and trust His grace,
I'll cast on Him my every care,
And wait for thee, sweet hour of prayer.

3 Sweet hour of prayer, sweet hour of prayer,
May I thy consolation share,
Till, from Mount Pisgah's lofty height,
I view my home, and take my flight:
This robe of flesh I'll drop, and rise
To seize the everlasting prize;
And shout, while passing through the air,
Farewell, farewell, sweet hour of prayer!

No. 73.   Retreat.

"I will commune with thee."—EX. 25 ; 22.

REV. HUGH STOWELL. DR. THOS. HASTINGS.

1. From ev'ry stormy wind that blows, From ev'ry swelling tide of woes,

There is a calm, a sure re-treat: 'Tis found beneath the mer-cy seat.

2 There is a place where Jesus sheds
The oil of gladness on our heads;
A place than all besides more sweet:
It is the blood-bought mercy-seat.

3 There is a scene where spirits blend,
Where friend holds fellowship with friend:

Tho' sundered far, by faith they meet
Around one common mercy-seat.

4 There, there on eagle wings we soar,
And sin and sense molest no more;
And heaven comes down our souls to greet,
While glory crowns the mercy-seat.

No. 74. What a Friend in Jesus.

"There is a friend that sticketh closer than a brother." — PROV. 18:24.

JOSEPH SCRIVEN.   C. C. CONVERSE, by per.

1. What a friend we have in Je-sus, All our sins and griefs to bear! What a priv-i-lege to car-ry Ev-erything to God in prayer! O, what peace we often for-feit, O, what needless pain we bear—All because we do not carry Everything to God in prayer!

2 Have we trials and temptations?
Is there trouble anywhere?
We should never be discouraged,
Take it to the Lord in prayer.
Can we find a friend so faithful
Who will all our sorrows share?
Jesus knows our every weakness.
Take it to the Lord in prayer.

3 Are we weak and heavy laden,
Cumbered with a load of care?
Precious Saviour! still our refuge,—
Take it to the Lord in prayer.
Do thy friends despise, forsake thee,
Take it to the Lord in prayer;
In His arms He'll take and shield thee,
Thou wilt find a solace there.

No. 75. Talmar.

"A friend loveth at all times." — PROV. 17:17.

REV. JOHN NEWTON.   I. B. WOODBURY.

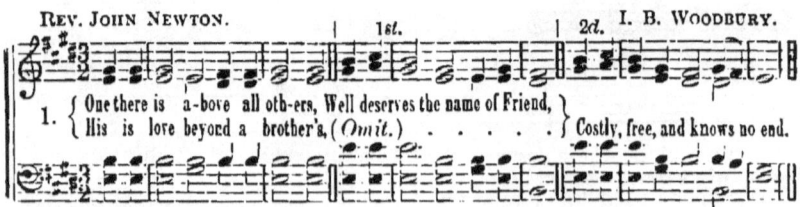

1. One there is a-bove all oth-ers, Well deserves the name of Friend,
His is love beyond a brother's, (*Omit.*) . . . . Costly, free, and knows no end.

2 Which of all our friends, to save us,
Could or would have shed his blood?
But our Jesus died to have us
Reconciled in Him to God.

3 O for grace our hearts to soften!
Teach us, Lord, at length to love;
We, alas! forget too often
What a friend we have above.

No. 76. The Mercy Seat.

"I will commune with thee from above the mercy-seat."—Ex. 25: 22.

G. J. F. W. H. DOANE.

1. Thou gracious Lord, enthroned above, Whose word is life, whose name is love;
   A - gain in bonds of un - ion sweet, We gather round the Mercy-seat.
   As once the cloud of glo-ry bright, O'er Israel shone by day and night,
   So let its beams our vis-ion greet, And cov-er now the Mer-cy-seat.

2. How oft in so - cial un-ion here, Thy hand has dried the falling tear;
   And ev - 'ry soul has felt how sweet To gather round the Mercy-seat.
   How oft this welcome hour has brought The precious boon our faith has sought;
   Our answered prayers have proved how sweet To gather round the Mer-cy-seat.

3. O hallowed hour, O blessed place, Where gently falls the dew of grace;
   And thou dost kind-ly deign to meet Thy children at the Mercy-seat.
   And while we humbly bend the knee, And lift our grateful hearts to Thee,
   There comes a truth divine-ly sweet, One faith, one Lord, one Mer-cy-seat.

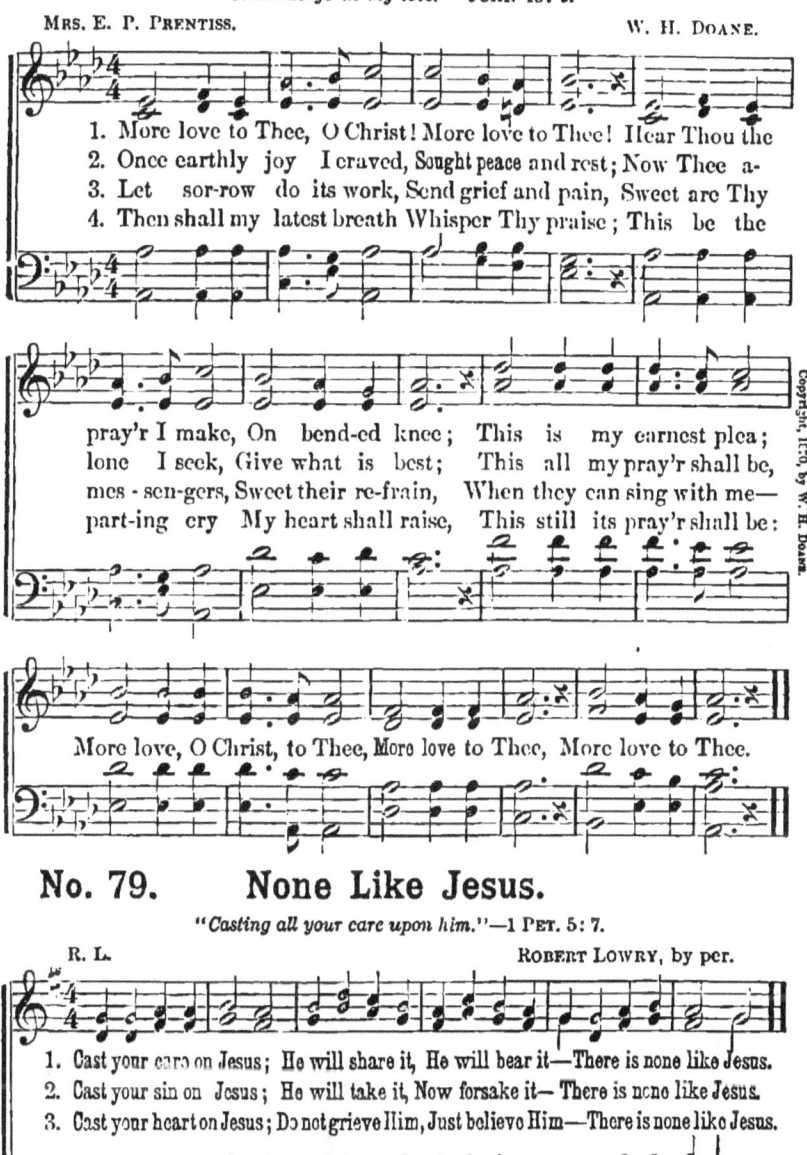

No. 82. I need Thee Every Hour.

"God shall supply all your need."—PHIL. 4: 19.

MRS. ANNIE S. HAWKS.   ROBERT LOWRY.

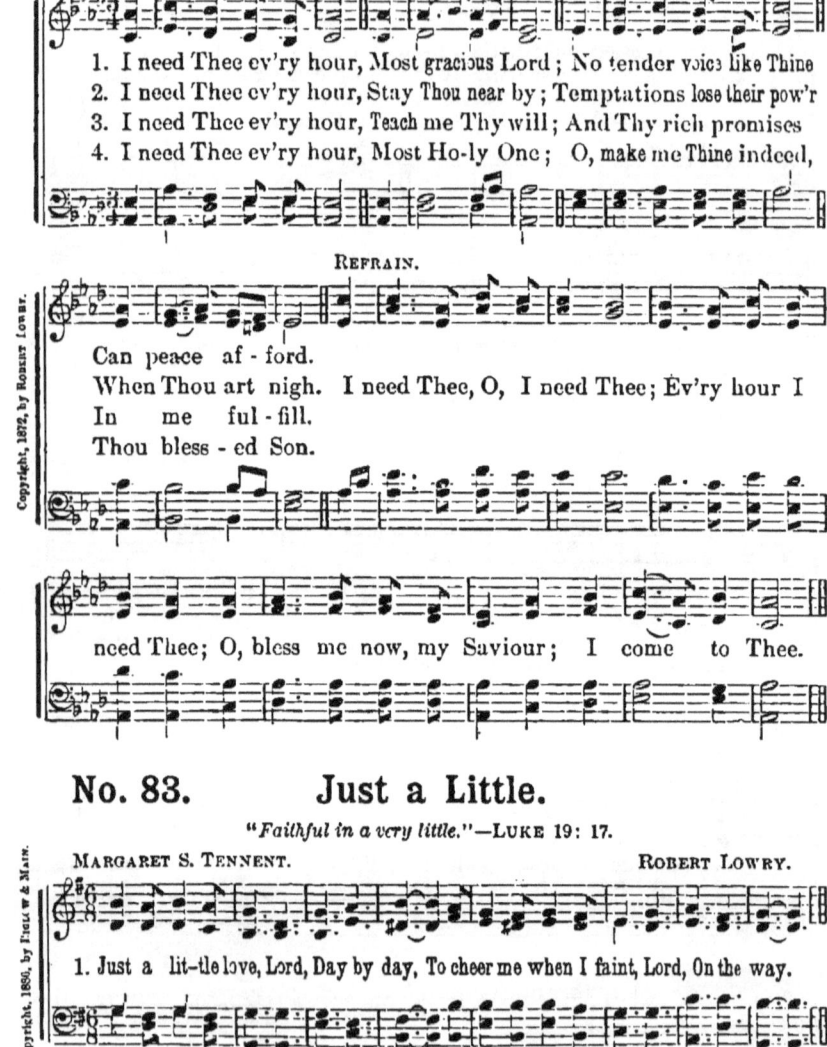

1. I need Thee ev'ry hour, Most gracious Lord; No tender voice like Thine
2. I need Thee ev'ry hour, Stay Thou near by; Temptations lose their pow'r
3. I need Thee ev'ry hour, Teach me Thy will; And Thy rich promises
4. I need Thee ev'ry hour, Most Ho-ly One; O, make me Thine indeed,

REFRAIN.

Can peace af - ford.
When Thou art nigh.   I need Thee, O, I need Thee; Ev'ry hour I
In me ful - fill.
Thou bless - ed Son.

need Thee; O, bless me now, my Saviour; I come to Thee.

Copyright, 1872, by ROBERT LOWRY.

No. 83. Just a Little.

"Faithful in a very little."—LUKE 19: 17.

MARGARET S. TENNENT.   ROBERT LOWRY.

1. Just a lit-tle love, Lord, Day by day, To cheer me when I faint, Lord, On the way.

2 Just a little faith, Lord,
   For a light
To guide me when I stray, Lord,
   In the night.

3 Just a little glimpse, Lord,
   Of yon shore,
To make me look and wish, Lord,
   Yet for more.

Copyright, 1880, by BIGLOW & MAIN.

75

No. 85. Draw Near, O Lord.

"Draw nigh unto my soul."—Ps. 69: 18.

R. L.   Robert Lowry.

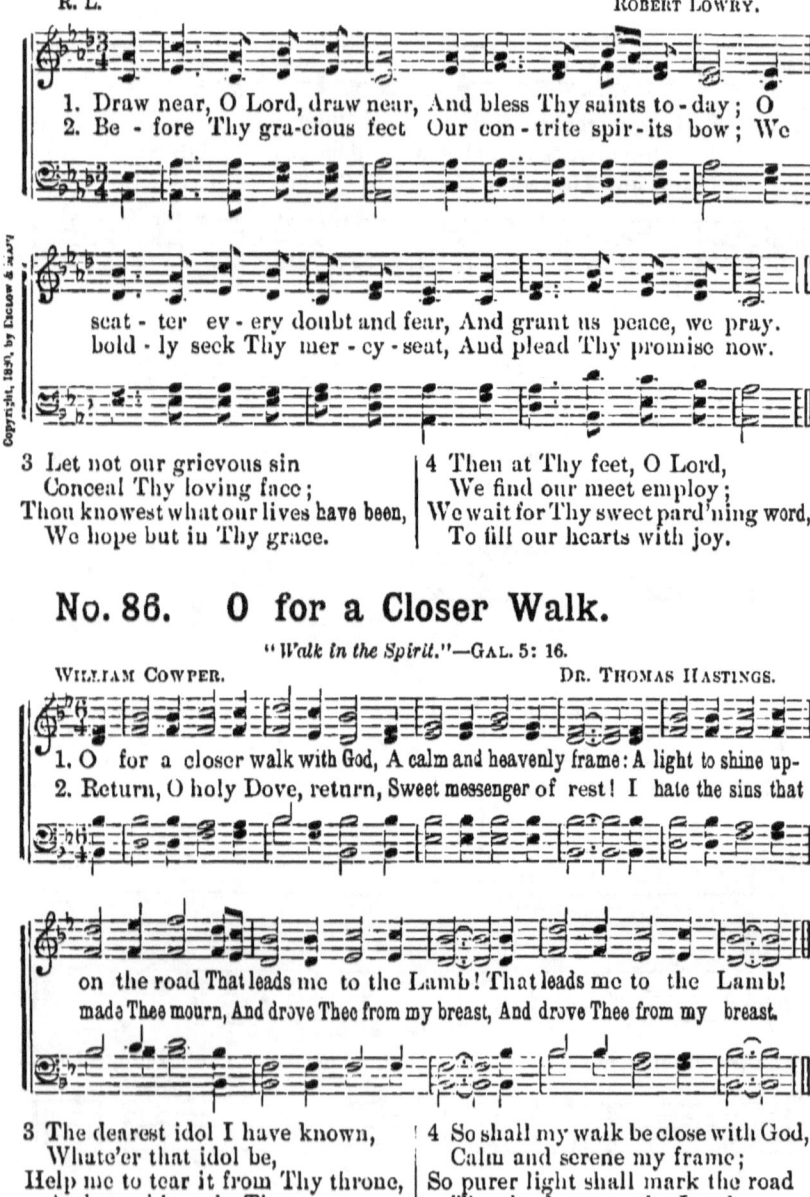

1. Draw near, O Lord, draw near, And bless Thy saints to-day; O scat-ter ev-ery doubt and fear, And grant us peace, we pray.
2. Be-fore Thy gra-cious feet Our con-trite spir-its bow; We bold-ly seek Thy mer-cy-seat, And plead Thy promise now.

3 Let not our grievous sin
   Conceal Thy loving face;
Thou knowest what our lives have been,
   We hope but in Thy grace.

4 Then at Thy feet, O Lord,
   We find our meet employ;
We wait for Thy sweet pard'ning word,
   To fill our hearts with joy.

No. 86. O for a Closer Walk.

"Walk in the Spirit."—Gal. 5: 16.

William Cowper.   Dr. Thomas Hastings.

1. O for a closer walk with God, A calm and heavenly frame: A light to shine up-on the road That leads me to the Lamb! That leads me to the Lamb!
2. Return, O holy Dove, return, Sweet messenger of rest! I hate the sins that made Thee mourn, And drove Thee from my breast, And drove Thee from my breast.

3 The dearest idol I have known,
   Whate'er that idol be,
Help me to tear it from Thy throne,
   And worship only Thee.

4 So shall my walk be close with God,
   Calm and serene my frame;
So purer light shall mark the road
   That leads me to the Lamb.

No. 87. I am the Lord's, and He is Mine.

"My beloved is mine, and I am his."—Sol. Song 2: 16.

Mrs. Annie S. Hawks.   Robert Lowry.

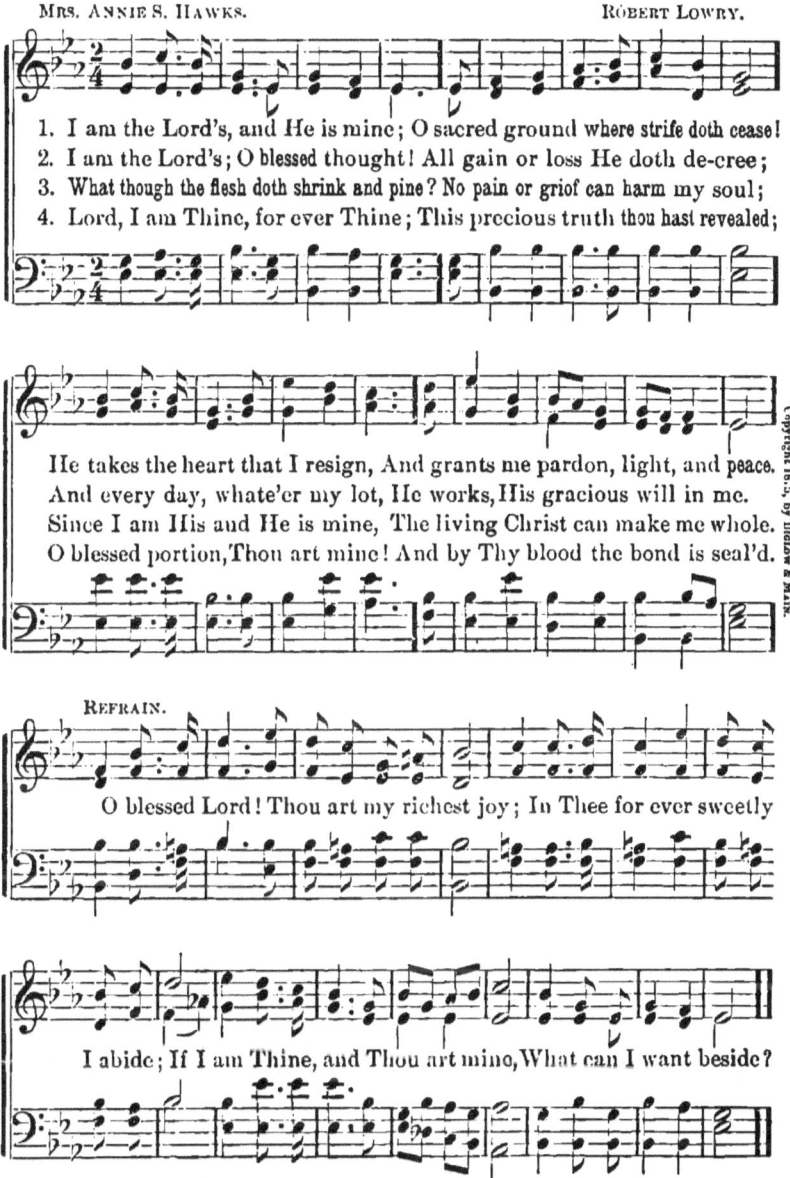

1. I am the Lord's, and He is mine; O sacred ground where strife doth cease!
2. I am the Lord's; O blessed thought! All gain or loss He doth de-cree;
3. What though the flesh doth shrink and pine? No pain or grief can harm my soul;
4. Lord, I am Thine, for ever Thine; This precious truth thou hast revealed;

He takes the heart that I resign, And grants me pardon, light, and peace.
And every day, whate'er my lot, He works, His gracious will in me.
Since I am His and He is mine, The living Christ can make me whole.
O blessed portion, Thou art mine! And by Thy blood the bond is seal'd.

REFRAIN.

O blessed Lord! Thou art my richest joy; In Thee for ever sweetly I abide; If I am Thine, and Thou art mine, What can I want beside?

Copyright 1875, by Biglow & Main.

No. 91. Deeper Love for Thee.

"Let my supplication come before thee."—Ps. 119: 170.

W. H. D.
W. H. DOANE.

1. Pre-cious Saviour, dear-est Friend, While we bend the knee,
2. Come and con-se-crate us now, Seal us ev - er Thine;
3. Trust-ing as a lit - tle child, Help us, Lord, to be,
4. Deep-er love, yes, deep-er love, This our con-stant plea;

Come and give our long-ing hearts Deep - er love to Thee.
May we to Thy ho - ly will Ev - ery power re - sign.
While we ask in sim - ple faith Deep - er love to Thee.
Deep-er love, yes, deep-er love, Till we're lost in Thee.

Copyright, 1880, by Biglow & Main.

REFRAIN.

Sav-iour, loving Redeemer, Saviour, precious to me, Grant me, I pray Thee, More of Thy Spirit, Drawing me clos-er, Clos-er to Thee.

82

No. 92. Wholly Thine.

"The very God of peace sanctify you wholly."—1 Thess. 5: 23.

Mrs. Annie S. Hawks.   Robert Lowry.

1. Thine, most gra-cious Lord, O make me whol-ly Thine—
2. Whol-ly Thine, my Lord, To go when Thou dost call;
3. Whol-ly Thine, O Lord, In ev-ery pass-ing hour;
4. Whol-ly Thine, O Lord, To fash-ion as Thou wilt,—
5. Thine, Lord, whol-ly Thine, For ev-er one with Thee—

Thine in thought, in word, and deed, For Thou, O Christ, art mine.
Thine to yield my ver-y self In all things, great and small.
Thine in si-lence, Thine to speak, As Thou dost grant the power.
Strengthen, bless and keep the soul Which Thou hast saved from guilt.
Root-ed, grounded in Thy love, A-bid-ing, sure and free.

Copyright, 1875, by Biglow & Main.

Refrain.

Whol-ly Thine, wholly Thine, Thou hast bought me, I am Thine;
Bless-ed Sav-iour, Thou art mine; Make me whol-ly Thine.

83

No. 94. Christ Receiveth Sinful Men.

"They that be whole need not a physician, but they that are sick." —MATT. 9:12.

From NEWMASTER. JAMES McGRANAHAN.

1. Sin-ners Je-sus will re-ceive; Sound this word of grace to all
   Who the heav'n-ly pathway leave, All who lin-ger, all who fall.
2. Come, and He will give you rest; Trust Him, for His word is plain;
   He will take the sin-ful-est; Christ re-ceiv-eth sin-ful men.
3. Now my heart condemns me not, Pure be-fore the law I stand;
   He who cleansed me from all spot, Sat-is-fied its last demand.
4. Christ re-ceiv-eth sin-ful men, E-ven me with all my sin;
   Purged from ev-'ry spot and stain, Heav'n with Him I en-ter in.

Copyright, 1882, by James McGranahan.

REFRAIN.

Sing it o'er . . . and o'er a-gain; . . . Christ re-
    Sing it o'er a-gain,   Sing it o'er a-gain;

ceiv - - - eth sin-ful men; . . .
ceiveth sinful men, Christ receiveth sinful men; Make the mes - - - sage
                                                  Make the message plain,

clear and plain: . . . . Christ re-ceiv-eth sin-ful men.
    Make the mes-sage plain;

No. 95. Only the Crumbs.

"—of the crumbs which fall." —MATT. 15: 27.

MRS. E. L PARK.   W. H. DOANE.

1. Sav-iour, behold in Thy mer-cy now, Hungry and poor at Thy
2. Sav-iour, I know, I am least of all, Yet to the feast I have
3. Ma-ny the souls Thou hast kindly fed, Here at Thy ta-ble so
4. On-ly the crumbs from Thy table give, On-ly the crumbs that my

feet I bow; Send me not hence or I faint and die, Hear Thou my cry.
heard Thy call; On-ly to gather the crumbs that fall, Glad I shall be.
rich-ly spread; On-ly the crumbs to receive from Thee, Blest I shall be.
soul may live; On-ly the crumbs would I ask of Thee, O, hear Thou me.

Copyright, 1889, by W. H. Doane.

REFRAIN.

On-ly the crumbs from Thy ta-ble, Lord, Bless-ed re-past for my soul will be; Only the crumbs from Thy table, Lord, Grant Thou to me.

No. 96. The Palace Gate of Prayer.

"Jesus himself drew near."—LUKE 24: 15.

D. B. P. D. B. PURINTON.

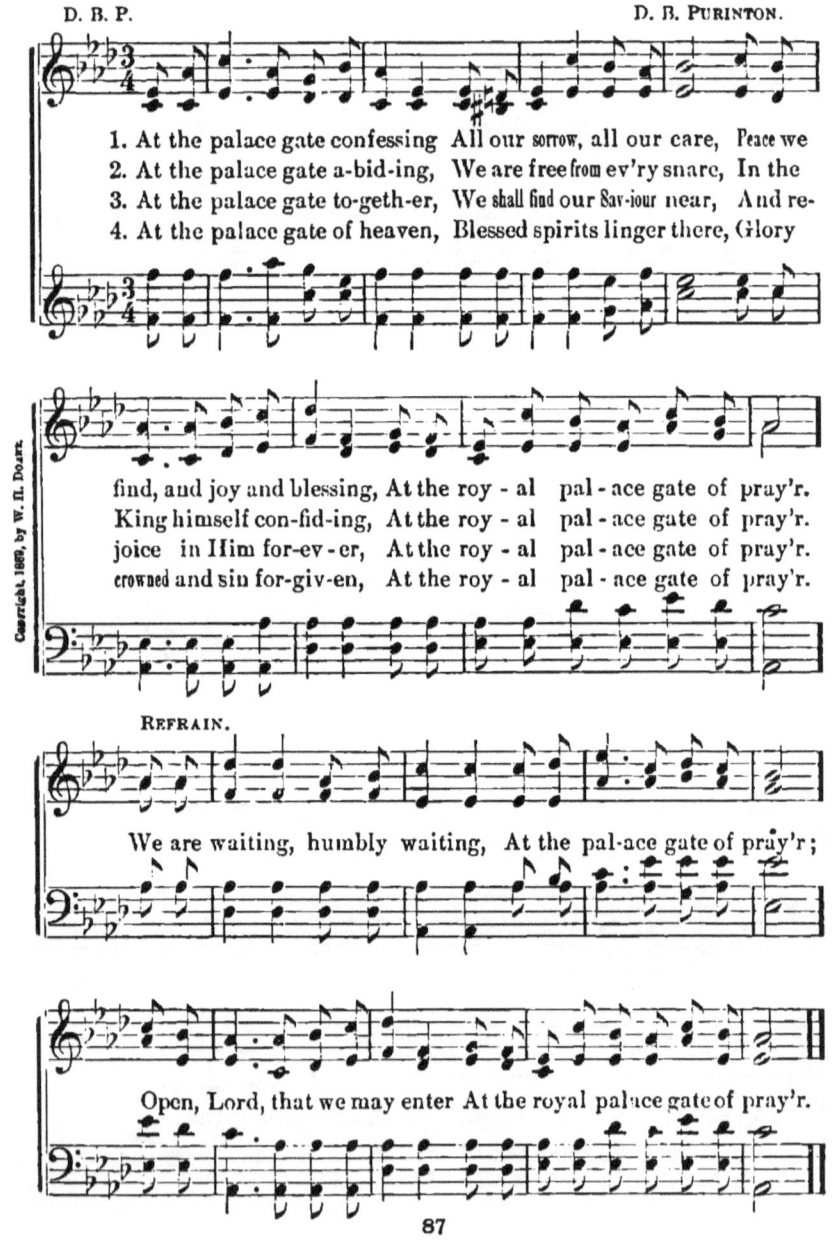

1. At the palace gate confessing All our sorrow, all our care, Peace we find, and joy and blessing, At the roy - al pal - ace gate of pray'r.
2. At the palace gate a-bid-ing, We are free from ev'ry snare, In the King himself con-fid-ing, At the roy - al pal - ace gate of pray'r.
3. At the palace gate to-geth-er, We shall find our Sav-iour near, And re-joice in Him for-ev-er, At the roy - al pal - ace gate of pray'r.
4. At the palace gate of heaven, Blessed spirits linger there, Glory crowned and sin for-giv-en, At the roy - al pal - ace gate of pray'r.

REFRAIN.

We are waiting, humbly waiting, At the pal-ace gate of pray'r;
Open, Lord, that we may enter At the royal palace gate of pray'r.

Dew of Mercy. Concluded.

how it cheers us, Ev-er fall-ing from a Saviour's love!
How it sweetly cheereth us!

No. 98. Jesus is Here.

"There am I in the midst of them." —MATT. 18: 20.

HELEN R. YOUNG. ROBERT LOWRY.

Copyright, 1888, by ROBERT LOWRY.

1. We stand on ho-ly ground— Je-sus is here;
2. Sal-va-tion now is nigh— Je-sus is here;
3. O bless-ed, hal-lowed hour— Je-sus is here;

His glo-ry shines a-round— Je-sus is here; The
O soul, for ref-uge fly— Je-sus is here; For
O day of sa-cred power— Je-sus is here; Come,

Lord is here to save and bless; O lost one, come, thy guilt con-
now in love He calls to thee, O wand'ring one, come un-to
has-ten now and seek His face, Believe His word of sovereign

fess; Be clothed with His own righteousness— Je-sus is here.
me; From sin's dark bondage now be free— Je-sus is here.
grace; The precious moments fly a-pace— Je-sus is here.

No. 99. Take the Promise.

"They shall never perish." —JOHN 10: 28.

R. L.
ROBERT LOWRY.

1. Take the promise as you go, Such as true be-lievers know;
2. What if round you falls the night? See the Day-star gleaming bright;
3. Child of faith, be firm, be strong; Heav'nly hopes to you belong;

Hide the word within your heart; Christ and you can nev-er part.
What if clouds obscure the day? Christ is with you all the way.
Tho' the earth be o-ver-thrown, Christ the Lord will know His own.

REFRAIN.

O Thou blessed Son of God, Help me walk where Thou hast trod:
Let Thy presence al-ways be Life and love and peace to me.

Copyright, 1884, by Biglow & Main.

No. 101. Rathbun.

"God forbid that I should glory, save in the cross." —GAL. 6: 14.

SIR JOHN BOWRING.   ITHAMAR CONKEY, by per.

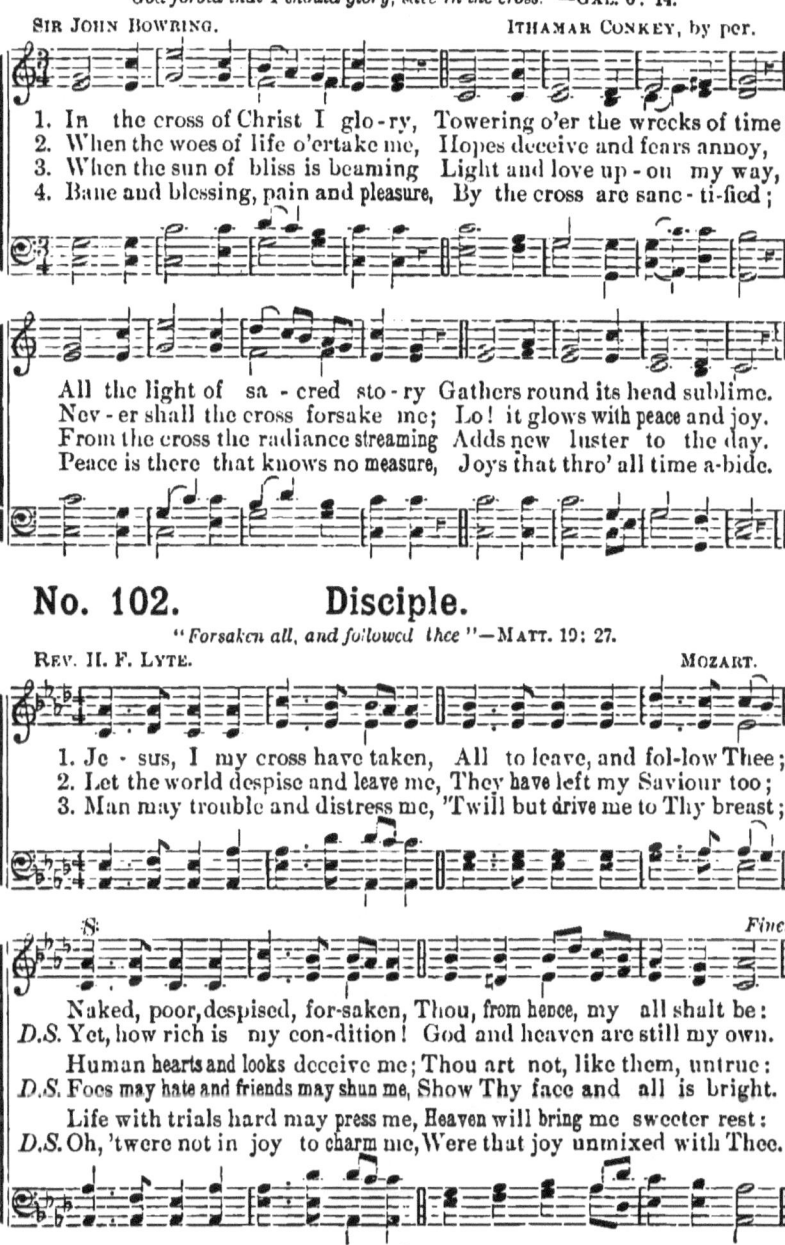

1. In the cross of Christ I glory, Towering o'er the wrecks of time;
2. When the woes of life o'ertake me, Hopes deceive and fears annoy,
3. When the sun of bliss is beaming Light and love up-on my way,
4. Bane and blessing, pain and pleasure, By the cross are sanc-ti-fied;

All the light of sa-cred sto-ry Gathers round its head sublime.
Nev-er shall the cross forsake me; Lo! it glows with peace and joy.
From the cross the radiance streaming Adds new luster to the day.
Peace is there that knows no measure, Joys that thro' all time a-bide.

No. 102. Disciple.

"Forsaken all, and followed thee" —MATT. 19: 27.

REV. H. F. LYTE.   MOZART.

1. Je-sus, I my cross have taken, All to leave, and fol-low Thee;
2. Let the world despise and leave me, They have left my Saviour too;
3. Man may trouble and distress me, 'Twill but drive me to Thy breast;

Naked, poor, despised, for-saken, Thou, from hence, my all shalt be:
D.S. Yet, how rich is my con-dition! God and heaven are still my own.

Human hearts and looks deceive me; Thou art not, like them, untrue:
D.S. Foes may hate and friends may shun me, Show Thy face and all is bright.

Life with trials hard may press me, Heaven will bring me sweeter rest:
D.S. Oh, 'twere not in joy to charm me, Were that joy unmixed with Thee.

Jesus, I My Cross. Concluded.

Per-ish ev-'ry fond am-bi-tion, All I've sought, or hoped, or known;
And while Thou shalt smile upon me, God of wis-dom, love and might,
Oh, 'tis not in grief to harm me While Thy love is left to me;

No. 103. Bear the Cross.

"On him they laid the cross."—LUKE 23: 26.

HELEN R. YOUNG.   ROBERT LOWRY.

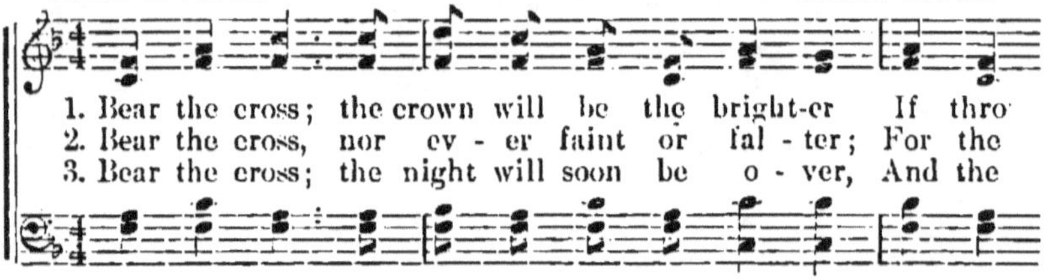

1. Bear the cross; the crown will be the bright-er If thro'
2. Bear the cross, nor ev-er faint or fal-ter; For the
3. Bear the cross; the night will soon be o-ver, And the

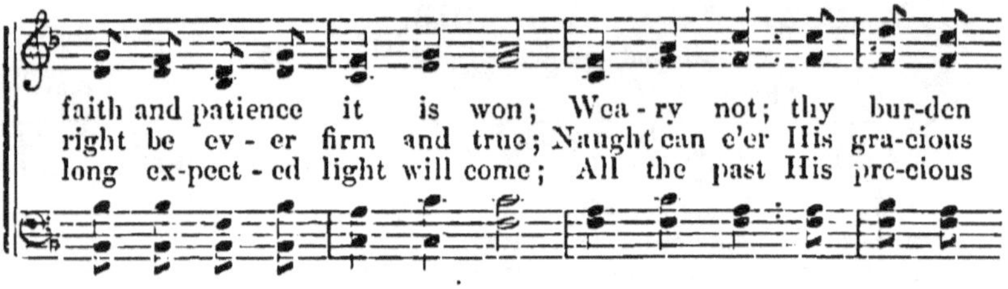

faith and patience it is won; Wea-ry not; thy bur-den
right be ev-er firm and true; Naught can e'er His gra-cious
long ex-pect-ed light will come; All the past His pre-cious

will seem light-er For the consciousness of du-ty done.
pur-pose al-ter, Who in ten-der love hath chos-en you.
love will cov-er With the joy of end-less rest and home.

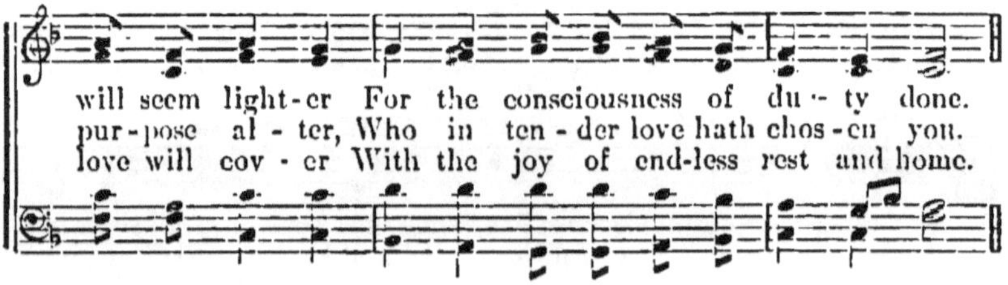

REFRAIN.

Bear the cross, bear the cross; All the brighter will be the crown.

No. 104. Just One Way.

"The way which leadeth unto life."—MATT. 7: 14.

A. J. HODGE. ROBERT LOWRY.

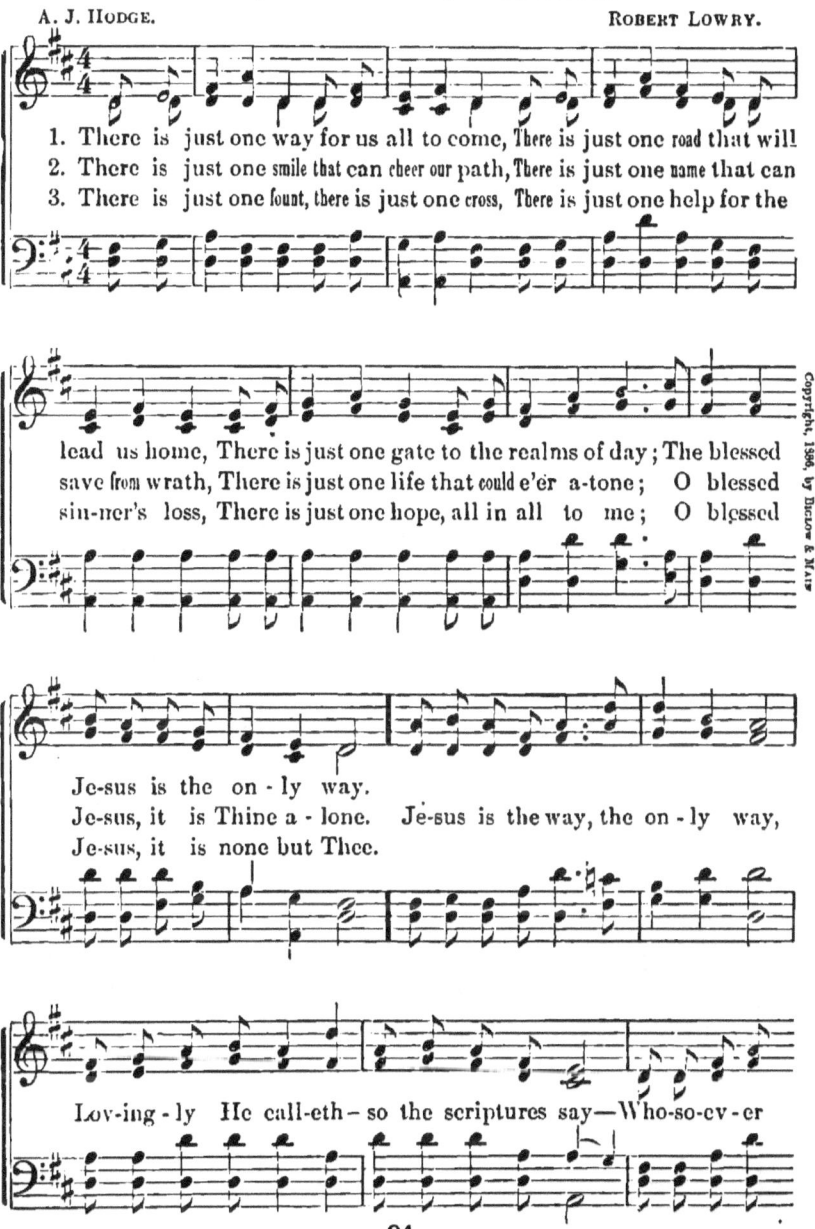

1. There is just one way for us all to come, There is just one road that will lead us home, There is just one gate to the realms of day; The blessed Jesus is the only way.
2. There is just one smile that can cheer our path, There is just one name that can save from wrath, There is just one life that could e'er a-tone; O blessed Jesus, it is Thine a-lone. Jesus is the way, the only way,
3. There is just one fount, there is just one cross, There is just one help for the sinner's loss, There is just one hope, all in all to me; O blessed Jesus, it is none but Thee.

Loving-ly He call-eth—so the scriptures say—Whosoever

Just One Way. Concluded.

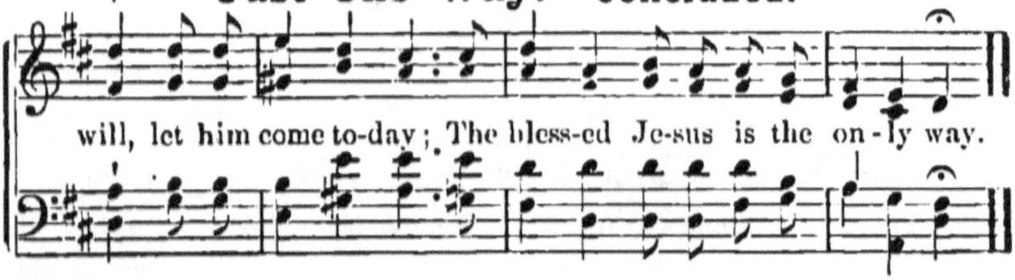

will, let him come to-day; The bless-ed Je-sus is the on-ly way.

No. 105. Lord, Keep Me Thine.

"I am thine."—Ps. 119: 94.

Mrs. F. J. Van Alstyne.   W. H. Doane.

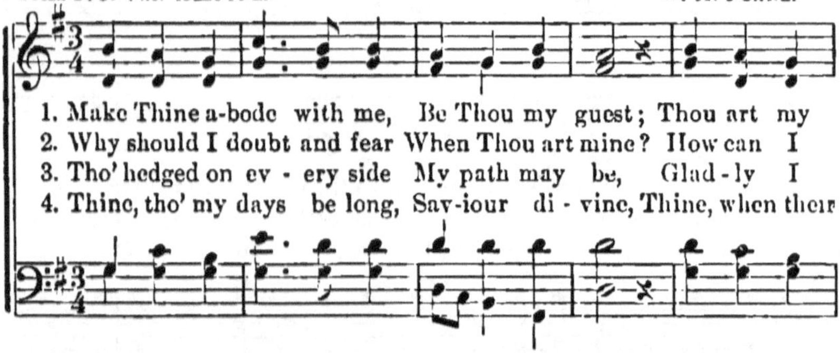

1. Make Thine a-bode with me, Be Thou my guest; Thou art my
2. Why should I doubt and fear When Thou art mine? How can I
3. Tho' hedged on ev - ery side My path may be, Glad - ly I
4. Thine, tho' my days be long, Sav-iour di - vine, Thine, when their

por - tion here, Thou art my rest; Tho', like a sum-mer day,
faint or fall, My hand in Thine? Light of my pil - grim way,
fol - low on, Trusting in Thee; Love, on ce - les - tial wings,
light shall fade, No more to shine; O Thou un-chang-ing Word,

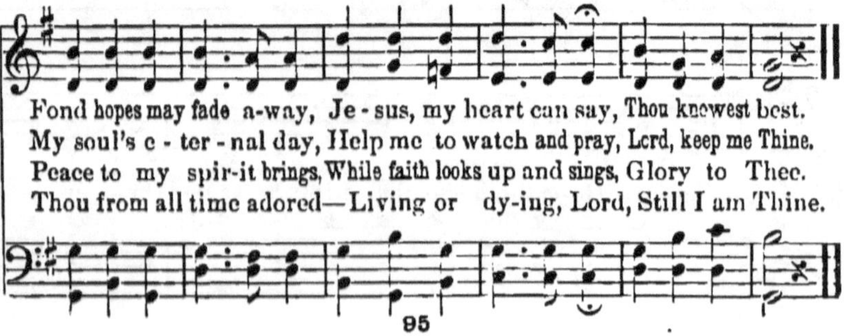

Fond hopes may fade a-way, Je - sus, my heart can say, Thou knowest best.
My soul's e - ter - nal day, Help me to watch and pray, Lord, keep me Thine.
Peace to my spir-it brings, While faith looks up and sings, Glory to Thee.
Thou from all time adored—Living or dy-ing, Lord, Still I am Thine.

No. 106. More Like Jesus.

"We shall be like him." 1 JOHN 3: 2.

F. J. C. W. H. DOANE.

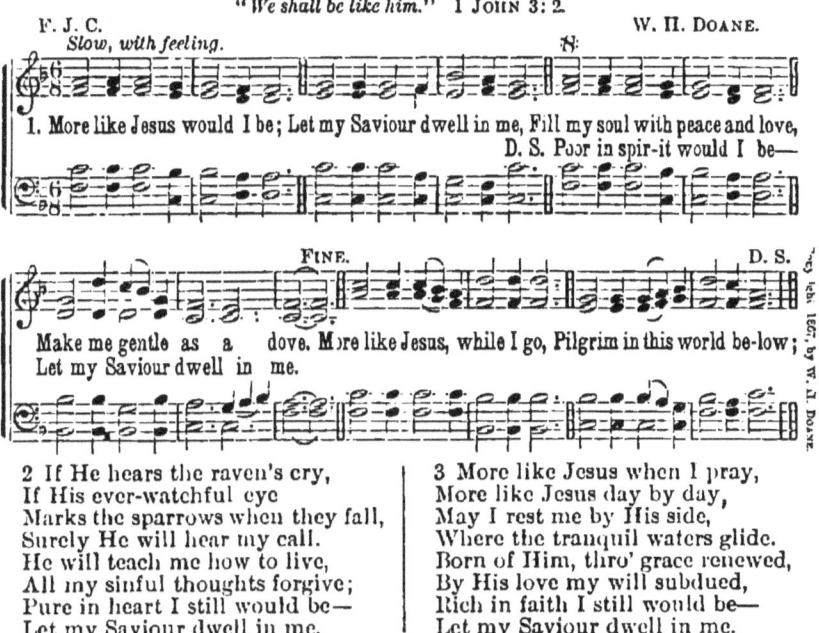

1. More like Jesus would I be; Let my Saviour dwell in me, Fill my soul with peace and love, Make me gentle as a dove. More like Jesus, while I go, Pilgrim in this world be-low; Poor in spir-it would I be— Let my Saviour dwell in me.

2 If He hears the raven's cry,
If His ever-watchful eye
Marks the sparrows when they fall,
Surely He will hear my call.
He will teach me how to live,
All my sinful thoughts forgive;
Pure in heart I still would be—
Let my Saviour dwell in me.

3 More like Jesus when I pray,
More like Jesus day by day,
May I rest me by His side,
Where the tranquil waters glide.
Born of Him, thro' grace renewed,
By His love my will subdued,
Rich in faith I still would be—
Let my Saviour dwell in me.

No. 107. Closer, Closer, Lord, to Thee.

"And the light shineth in darkness."—JOHN 1: 5.

MRS. CHARLOTTE B. MERRITT. ROBERT LOWRY.

1. Closer, closer, Lord, to Thee, While the tempest rages wild; Thro' the darkness of the storm, Take Thy sad and sinful child. Closer, closer, Lord, to Thee, Till Thy face in heaven I see.

2 Lead me on to glorious light,
Where the clouds all melt away;
Where the ever constant sun
Makes and keeps a perfect day.

3 O Thou Sun of Righteousness,
Shining with Thy perfect ray.
Lead me on through paths of peace,
To the never-ending day.

No. 108. Sun of My Soul.

"Abide in me, and I in you."—JOHN 15: 4.

REV. JOHN KEBLE. PETER RITTER.

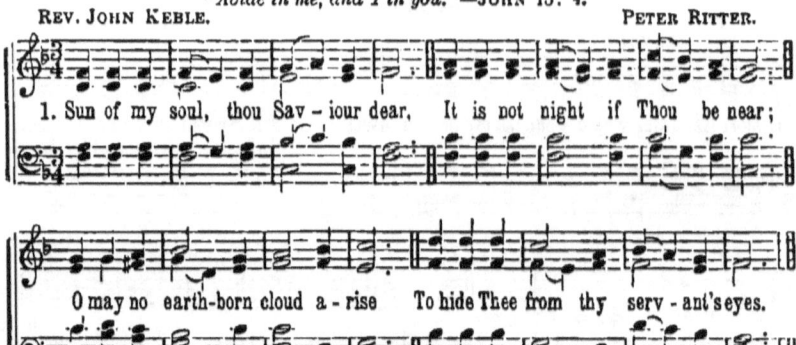

1. Sun of my soul, thou Saviour dear, It is not night if Thou be near;
O may no earth-born cloud arise To hide Thee from thy servant's eyes.

2 When the soft dews of kindly sleep
My wearied eyelids gently steep,
Be my last thought, how sweet to rest
Forever on my Saviour's breast!

3 Abide with me from morn till eve,
For without Thee I can not live;

Abide with me when night is nigh,
For without Thee I dare not die.

4 Come near and bless us when we wake,
Ere through the world our way we take;
Till, in the ocean of Thy love,
We lose ourselves in heaven above.

No. 109. Abide with Me.

"Abide with us."—LUKE 24: 29.

REV. H. F. LYTE. W. H. MONK.

1. Abide with me; fast falls the eventide; The darkness deepens—Lord, with me abide;
When helpers fail, and other comforts flee, Help of the helpless, O abide with me!

2 Swift to its close ebbs out life's little day;
Earth's joys grow dim, its glories pass away;
Change and decay in all around I see;
O Thou who changest not, abide with me!

3 Hold Thou Thy cross before my closing eyes;
Shine through the gloom, and point me to the skies;
Heaven's morning breaks, and earth's vain shadows flee;
In life, in death, O Lord, abide with me!

No. 110. O Thou that Hearest Prayer.

"O thou that hearest prayer."—Is. 65: 2.

FANNY J. CROSBY.   W. H. DOANE.

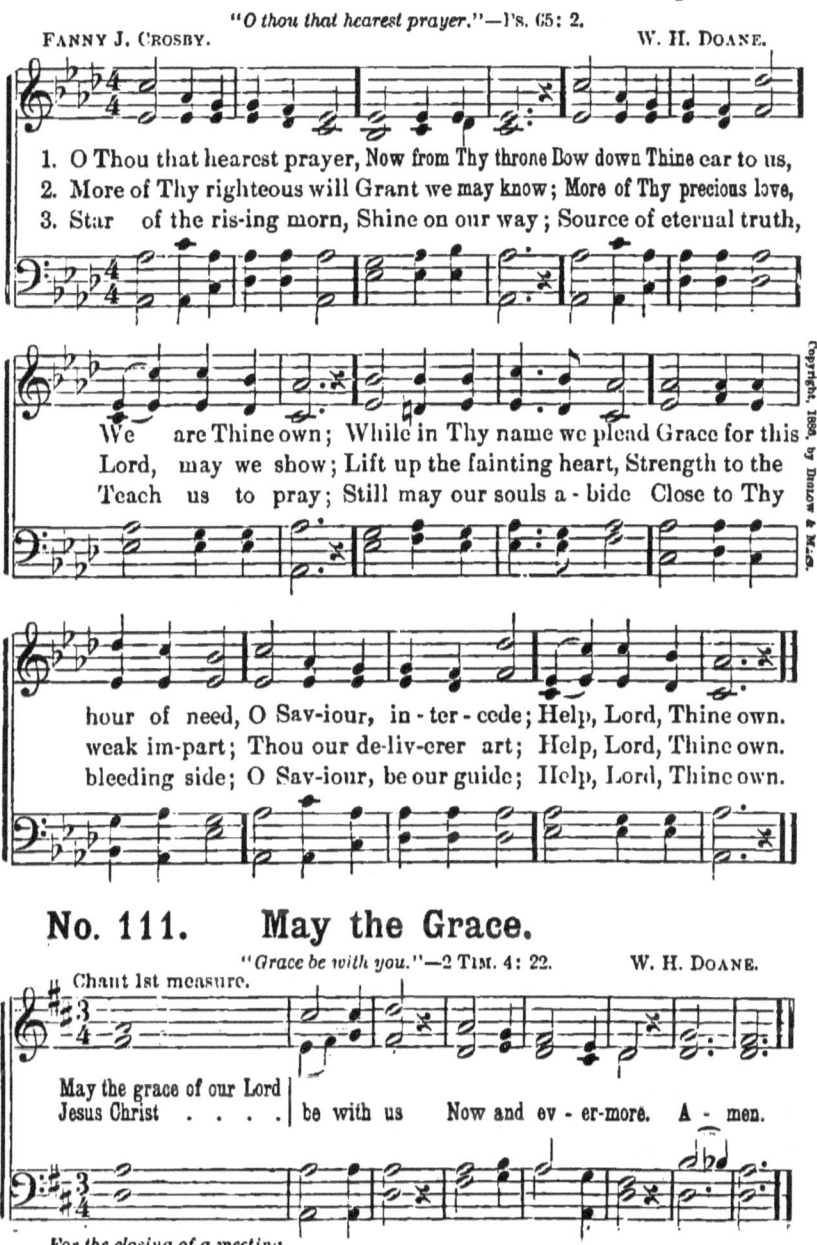

1. O Thou that hearest prayer, Now from Thy throne Bow down Thine ear to us, We are Thine own; While in Thy name we plead Grace for this hour of need, O Sav-iour, in-ter-cede; Help, Lord, Thine own.
2. More of Thy righteous will Grant we may know; More of Thy precious love, Lord, may we show; Lift up the fainting heart, Strength to the weak im-part; Thou our de-liv-erer art; Help, Lord, Thine own.
3. Star of the ris-ing morn, Shine on our way; Source of eternal truth, Teach us to pray; Still may our souls a-bide Close to Thy bleeding side; O Sav-iour, be our guide; Help, Lord, Thine own.

No. 111. May the Grace.

"Grace be with you."—2 Tim. 4: 22.

W. H. DOANE.

Chant 1st measure.

May the grace of our Lord Jesus Christ . . . . | be with us Now and ev-er-more. A-men.

For the closing of a meeting.

98

No. 112. Jesus, I Love Thee.

Rev. John Love, Jr.   *"I am with you alway."*—Matt. 28: 20.   Robert Lowry.

1. Je-sus, I love Thee, Thou art my dearest friend; With me, till life shall end, Gra-cious-ly be; Thy promise I be-lieve, Thy peace let me receive, Heaven's choicest blessings give, Saviour, to me.
2. Je-sus, I trust Thee, Why should I know a fear, Since Thou to me so near Ev-er wilt be? My heav-y burdens share, Help me my griefs to bear, Bring me, thro' ev'ry care, Closer to Thee.
3. Je-sus, I need Thee All thro' life's wea-ry way; O grant me still, I pray, Grace full and free; So shall I ne'er re-pine, Each woe will but refine; Make me entirely Thine, Saviour, to be.

No. 113. Trust in God, My Brother.

E. A. Barnes.   *"Trust in the mercy of God."*—Psa. 52: 8.   Robert Lowry.

1. Trust in God, my brother, All the days to come; Let your simple faith in Him Guide you to His Home.

Ref.—Trust Him as a Father, Trust Him as a Friend, Trust Him as a Refuge sure, Trust Him to the end.

2 Trust in God, my brother,
With a spirit true;
All His ways are just and right,
And He cares for you.

3 Trust in God, my brother,
Till He bring you home,
Till your trials all shall cease
In the life to come.

No. 114. Expostulation.

REV. JOSIAH HOPKINS. *"Turn to the Lord."*—Hos. 14: 2. REV. JOSIAH HOPKINS.

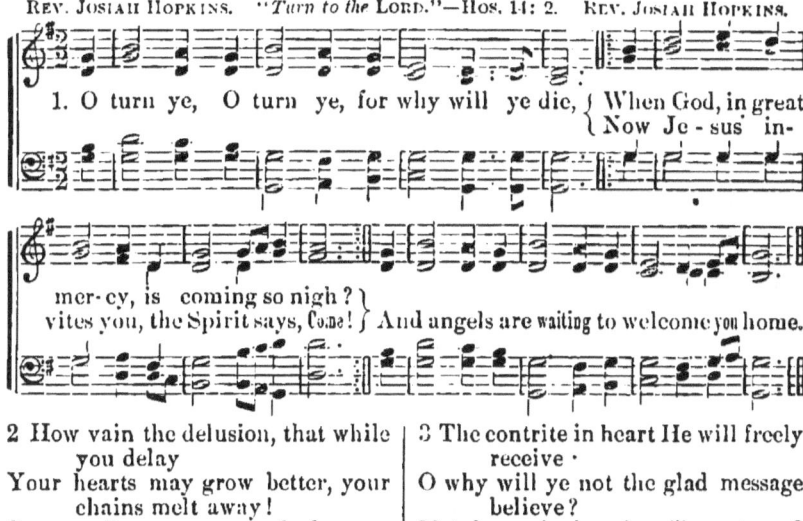

1. O turn ye, O turn ye, for why will ye die, { When God, in great mer-cy, is coming so nigh? { Now Je-sus in-vites you, the Spirit says, Come! } And angels are waiting to welcome you home.

2 How vain the delusion, that while you delay
Your hearts may grow better, your chains melt away!
Come guilty, come wretched, come just as you are;
All helpless and dying to Jesus repair.

3 The contrite in heart He will freely receive ·
O why will ye not the glad message believe?
If sin be your burden, why will ye not come?
'Tis you He makes welcome; He bids you come home.

No. 115. Come, Ye Sinners.

"Come, and let us return unto the Lord."—Hos. 6: 1.

REV. JOSEPH HART. J. INGALLS.

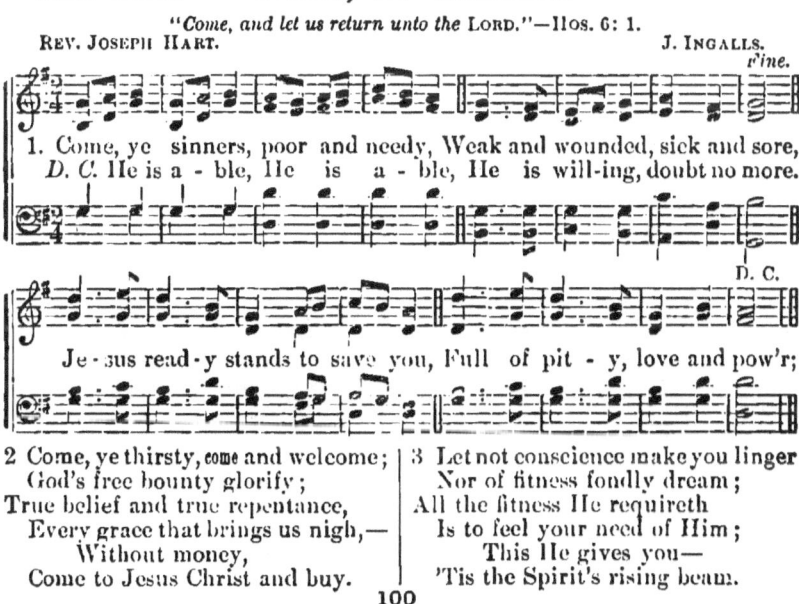

1. Come, ye sinners, poor and needy, Weak and wounded, sick and sore,
D. C. He is a-ble, He is a-ble, He is will-ing, doubt no more.
Je-sus read-y stands to save you, Full of pit-y, love and pow'r;

2 Come, ye thirsty, come and welcome;
God's free bounty glorify;
True belief and true repentance,
Every grace that brings us nigh,—
Without money,
Come to Jesus Christ and buy.

3 Let not conscience make you linger
Nor of fitness fondly dream;
All the fitness He requireth
Is to feel your need of Him;
This He gives you,
'Tis the Spirit's rising beam.

No. 116. Lord, in Thy Name.

"I have remembered thy name."—Ps. 119: 55.

W. H. D.   W. H. DOANE.

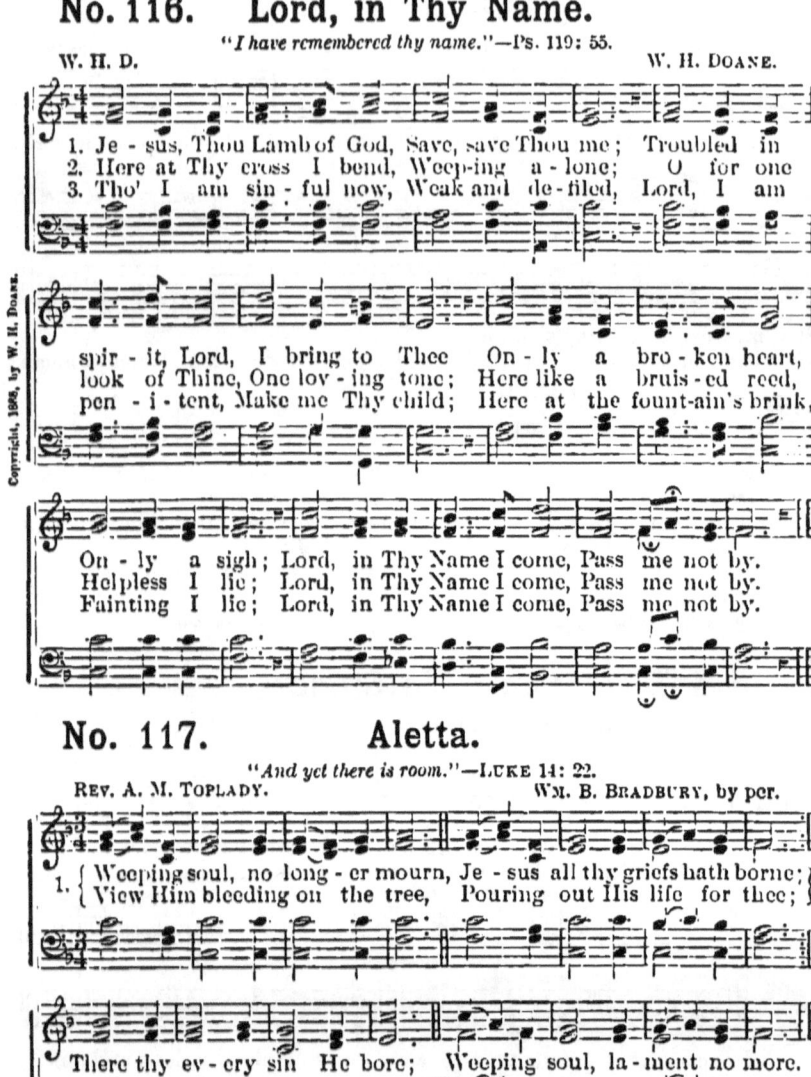

1. Je-sus, Thou Lamb of God, Save, save Thou me; Troubled in spir-it, Lord, I bring to Thee On-ly a bro-ken heart, On-ly a sigh; Lord, in Thy Name I come, Pass me not by.
2. Here at Thy cross I bend, Weep-ing a-lone; O for one look of Thine, One lov-ing tone; Here like a bruis-ed reed, Helpless I lie; Lord, in Thy Name I come, Pass me not by.
3. Tho' I am sin-ful now, Weak and de-filed, Lord, I am pen-i-tent, Make me Thy child; Here at the fount-ain's brink, Fainting I lie; Lord, in Thy Name I come, Pass me not by.

No. 117. Aletta.

"And yet there is room."—LUKE 14: 22.

REV. A. M. TOPLADY.   WM. B. BRADBURY, by per.

1. Weeping soul, no long-er mourn, Je-sus all thy griefs hath borne;
View Him bleeding on the tree, Pouring out His life for thee;
There thy ev-ery sin He bore; Weeping soul, la-ment no more.

2 Cast thy guilty soul on Him,
Find Him mighty to redeem;
At His feet Thy burden lay,
Look thy doubts and fears away;
Now by faith the Son embrace,
Plead His promise, trust His grace.

3 Lord, Thy arm must be revealed,
Ere I can by faith be healed;
Since I scarce can look to Thee,
Cast a gracious eye on me;
At Thy feet myself I lay;
Shine, O shine my sins away.

No. 118. Nothing but the Blood.

"Without shedding of blood is no remission."—Heb. 9: 22.

R. L.   Robert Lowry.

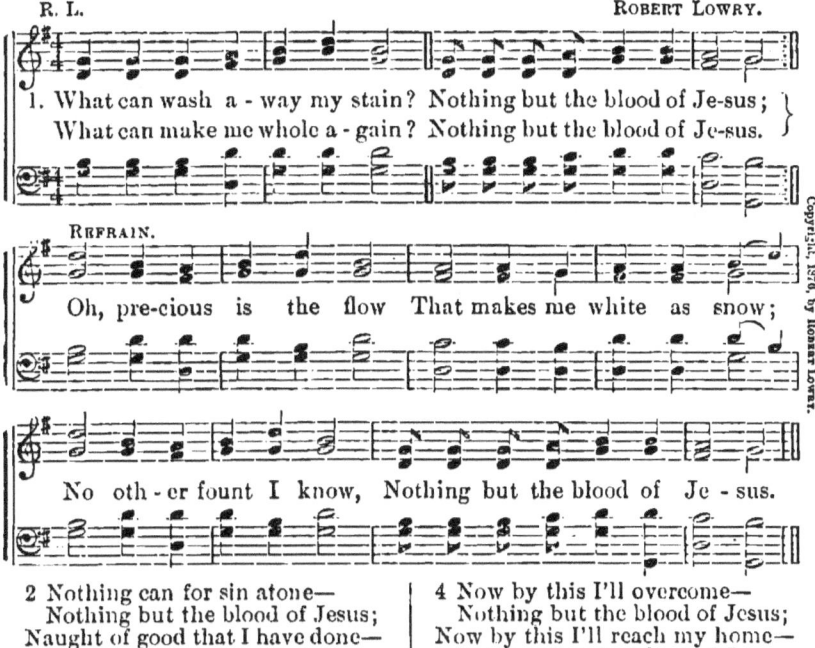

1. What can wash a-way my stain? Nothing but the blood of Je-sus;
What can make me whole a-gain? Nothing but the blood of Je-sus.

REFRAIN.
Oh, pre-cious is the flow That makes me white as snow;
No oth-er fount I know, Nothing but the blood of Je-sus.

Copyright, 1876, by Robert Lowry.

2 Nothing can for sin atone—
Nothing but the blood of Jesus;
Naught of good that I have done—
Nothing but the blood of Jesus.

3 This is all my hope and peace—
Nothing but the blood of Jesus
This is all my righteousness—
Nothing but the blood of Jesus.

4 Now by this I'll overcome—
Nothing but the blood of Jesus;
Now by this I'll reach my home—
Nothing but the blood of Jesus.

5 Glory! glory! thus I sing—
Nothing but the blood of Jesus;
All my praise for this I bring—
Nothing but the blood of Jesus.

No. 119. To-day the Saviour Calls.

"If ye seek him, he will be found of you."—2 Chron. 15: 2.

S. F. Smith.   Dr. Lowell Mason.

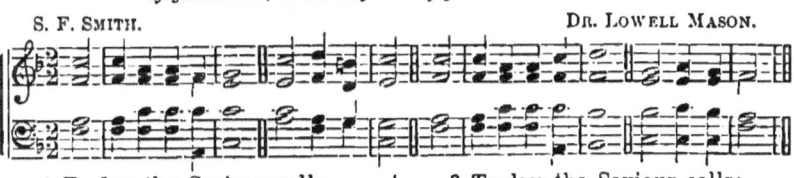

1 To-day the Saviour calls;
Ye wanderers, come;
O, ye benighted souls,
Why longer roam?

2 To-day the Saviour calls;
O, hear Him now;
Within these sacred walls
To Jesus bow.

3 To-day the Saviour calls;
For refuge fly;
The storm of justice falls,
And death is nigh.

4 The Spirit calls to-day;
Yield to His power;
O, grieve Him not away;
'Tis mercy's hour.

No. 120. Pass Me Not.

"*Whosoever shall call upon the name of the Lord shall be saved.*"—Rom. 10: 13.

FANNY J. CROSBY.   W. H. DOANE.

1. Pass me not, O gen-tle Sav-iour, Hear my hum-ble cry;
2. Let me at Thy throne of mer-cy Find a sweet re-lief;
3. Trust-ing on-ly in Thy mer-its, Would I seek Thy face;
4. Thou, the spring of all my com-fort, More than life to me—

While on oth-ers Thou art smil-ing, Do not pass me by.
Kneel-ing there in deep con-tri-tion, Help my un-be-lief.
Heal my wounded, bro-ken spir-it, Save me by Thy grace.
Whom have I on earth be-side Thee? Whom in heaven but Thee?

D.S. *While on oth-ers Thou art call-ing, Do not pass me by.*

REFRAIN.

Sav-iour, Sav-iour, Hear my hum-ble cry;

Copyright, 1870, by W. H. DOANE.

No. 121. Even Me.

"*There shall be showers of blessing.*"—Ezek. 34: 26.

MRS. ELIZABETH CODNER.   WM. B. BRADBURY.

1. { Lord, I hear of show'rs of blessing Thou art scatt'ring full and free—
    Show'rs the thirsty land refreshing; Let some droppings fall on me—}

REFRAIN.

Even me, e-ven me, Let some droppings fall on me.

2 Pass me not, O God, my Father!
  Sinful though my heart may be;
  Thou might'st leave me, but the rather
  Let Thy mercy light on me.

3 Pass me not, O gracious Saviour!
  Let me live and cling to Thee;
  For I'm longing for Thy favor;
  Whilst Thou'rt calling, O call me.

Copyright, 1862, by W. B. BRADBURY.

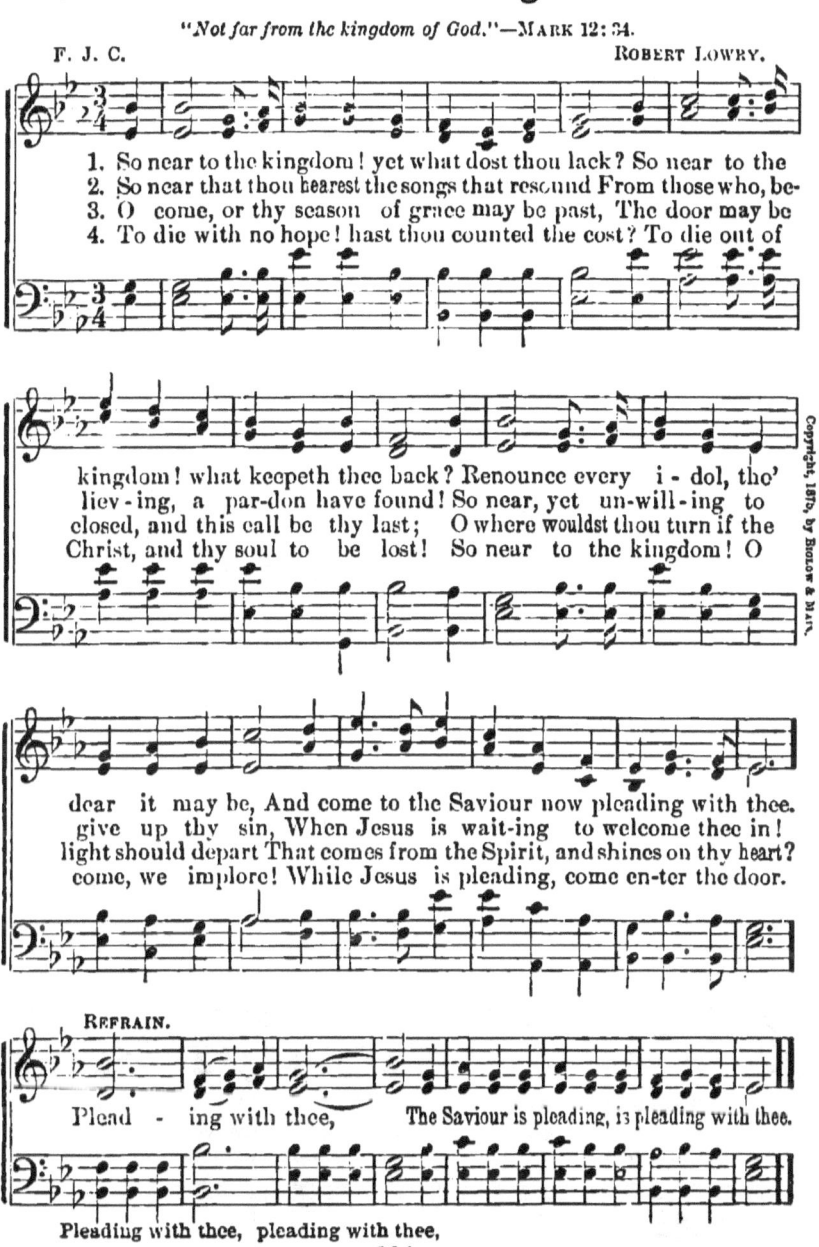

No. 123. Though your Sins be as Scarlet.

"Though your sins be as scarlet, they shall be as white as snow."—Is. 1: 18.

FANNY J. CROSBY. (SPECIAL OCCASIONS.) W. H. DOANE.

DUET. *Gently.*

1. "Tho' your sins be as scarlet, They shall be as white as snow; as snow;
2. Hear the voice that entreats you, Oh, re-turn ye un-to God! to God!
3. He'll forgive your transgressions, And remember them no more; no more;

QUARTET.

Tho' they be red . . . . . like crim-son, They shall be as wool;"
He is of great . . . . . com-pas-sion, And of wond'rous love;
"Look un-to Me, ... ye people," Saith the Lord your God;

Tho' they be red

DUET. *p*   QUARTET. *f*

"Tho' your sins be as scar-let, Tho' your sins be as scar-let,
Hear the voice that entreats you, Hear the voice that en-treats you,
He'll for-give your transgressions, He'll for-give your transgressions,

p Rit.

They shall be as white as snow, They shall be as white as snow."
Oh, re-turn ye un-to God! Oh, re-turn ye un-to God!
And re-mem-ber them no more, And re-mem-ber them no more.

Copyright, 1875, by W. H. DOANE.

No. 129. Who'll be the Next?

"If any man serve me, let him follow me." — JOHN 12: 26.

MRS. ANNIE S. HAWKS.   ROBERT LOWRY.

1. Who'll be the next to fol - low Je - sus? Who'll be the next His cross to bear? Some one is read - y, some one is wait - ing;
2. Who'll be the next to fol - low Je - sus — Fol - low His wea - ry, bleed-ing feet? Who'll be the next to lay ev - 'ry bur - den
3. Who'll be the next to fol - low Je - sus? Who'll be the next to praise His name? Who'll swell the cho - rus of free re - demption —
4. Who'll be the next to fol - low Je - sus Down thro' the Jor - dan's roll - ing tide? Who'll be the next to join with the ran-somed,

REFRAIN.

Who'll be the next a crown to wear?
Down at the Fa - ther's mer - cy seat? Who'll be the next?
Sing, Hal - le - lu - jah! praise the Lamb?
Sing - ing up - on the oth - er side?

Who'll be the next? Who'll be the next to fol - low Je - sus? Who'll be the next to fol - low Je - sus now? Fol - low Je - sus now.

Copyright, 1871, by Biglow & Main.

No. 131. The Royal Message.

"I have a message from God unto thee."—JUDGES 3: 20.

M. LOWRIE HOFFORD, D. D. W. H. DOANE.

1. I have a roy-al mes-sage, Thro' yon-der arch it rings,
2. I have a ten-der mes-sage From Christ, your dearest friend:
3. I have a lov-ing mes-sage: Come un-to me and rest;

With ti-dings, joy-ful ti-dings, From Christ the King of kings.
My pres-ence shall go with you, Be with you to the end.
Ye who are heav-y la-den, Find shel-ter on my breast.

Copyright, 1886, by BIGLOW & MAIN.

REFRAIN.

A-bund-ant life He of-fers; Then at His al-tar bow;

E-ter-nal life He gives you—Ac-cept, ac-cept it now.

No. 132. Weeping Will Not Save Me.

"For by grace are ye saved through faith."—Eph. 2: 8.

R. L.
Robert Lowry.

1. Weeping will not save me—Tho' my face were bathed in tears,
2. Working will not save me—Pur-est deeds that I can do,
3. Waiting will not save me—Helpless, guilt-y, lost I lie,
4. Faith in Christ will save me—Let me trust Thy weeping Son,

That could not al-lay my fears, Could not wash the sins of years—
Hol-iest thoughts and feelings too, Can-not form my soul a-new—
In my ear is mer-cy's cry; If I wait I can but die—
Trust the work that He has done; To His arms, Lord, help me run—

REFRAIN.

Weeping will not save me.
Working will not save me. Jesus wept and died for me; Jesus suffered
Wait-ing will not save me.
Faith in Christ will save me.

on the tree; Jesus waits to make me free: He a-lone can save me.

No. 133. Jesus Saves!

"Believe on the Lord Jesus Christ, and thou shalt be saved."—Acts 16: 31.

PRISCILLA J. OWENS.   WM. J. KIRKPATRICK, by per.

1. We have heard the joy-ful sound: Je-sus saves! Je-sus saves!
2. Waft it on the roll-ing tide: Je-sus saves! Je-sus saves!
3. Sing a-bove the bat-tle strife: Je-sus saves! Je-sus saves!
4. Give the winds a might-y voice: Je-sus saves! Je-sus saves!

Spread the ti-dings all a-round: Je-sus saves! Je-sus saves!
Tell to sin-ners far and wide: Je-sus saves! Je-sus saves!
By His death and end-less life, Je-sus saves! Je-sus saves!
Let the na-tions now re-joice: Je-sus saves! Je-sus saves!

Bear the news to ev-'ry land, Climb the steeps and cross the waves;
Sing, ye isl-ands of the sea, Ech-o back, ye o-cean caves;
Sing it soft-ly thro' the gloom, When the heart for mer-cy craves;
Shout sal-va-tion full and free, High-est hills and deep-est caves;

On-ward!—'tis our Lord's command: Je-sus saves! Je-sus saves!
Earth shall keep her ju-bi-lee: Je-sus saves! Je-sus saves!
Sing in tri-umph o'er the tomb,— Je-sus saves! Je-sus saves!
This our song of vic-to-ry,— Je-sus saves! Je-sus saves!

No. 134. Redeeming Work.

"He sent redemption unto His people."—Ps. 111:9.

MRS. F. J. V. A. JOHN T. GRAPE, by per.

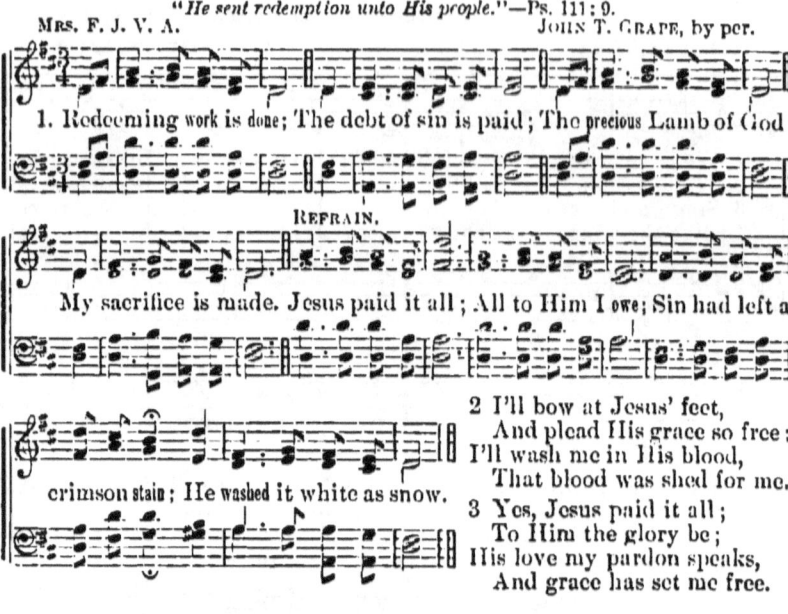

1. Redeeming work is done; The debt of sin is paid; The precious Lamb of God My sacrifice is made. Jesus paid it all; All to Him I owe; Sin had left a crimson stain; He washed it white as snow.

2 I'll bow at Jesus' feet,
And plead His grace so free;
I'll wash me in His blood,
That blood was shed for me.

3 Yes, Jesus paid it all;
To Him the glory be;
His love my pardon speaks,
And grace has set me free.

No. 135. Just as I Am.

"We have redemption through his blood."—EPH. 1:7.

MISS CHARLOTTE ELLIOTT. WM. B. BRADBURY, by per.

1. Just as I am, without one plea But that Thy blood was shed for me, And that Thou bid'st me come to Thee, O Lamb of God, I come, I come!

2 Just as I am, and waiting not
To rid my soul of one dark blot,
To Thee, whose blood can cleanse each spot,
O Lamb of God, I come, I come!

3 Just as I am, tho' tossed about
With many a conflict, many a doubt,
Fightings within, and fears without,
O Lamb of God, I come, I come!

4 Just as I am,—Thou wilt receive,
Wilt welcome, pardon, cleanse, relieve;
Because Thy promise I believe,
O Lamb of God, I come, I come!

5 Just as I am,—Thy love unknown
Has broken every barrier down;
Now, to be Thine, yea, Thine alone,
O Lamb of God, I come, I come!

No. 136. Why Do You Wait?

"Come thou, for there is peace to thee."—1 Sam. 20: 21.

G. F. R.
Geo. F. Root.

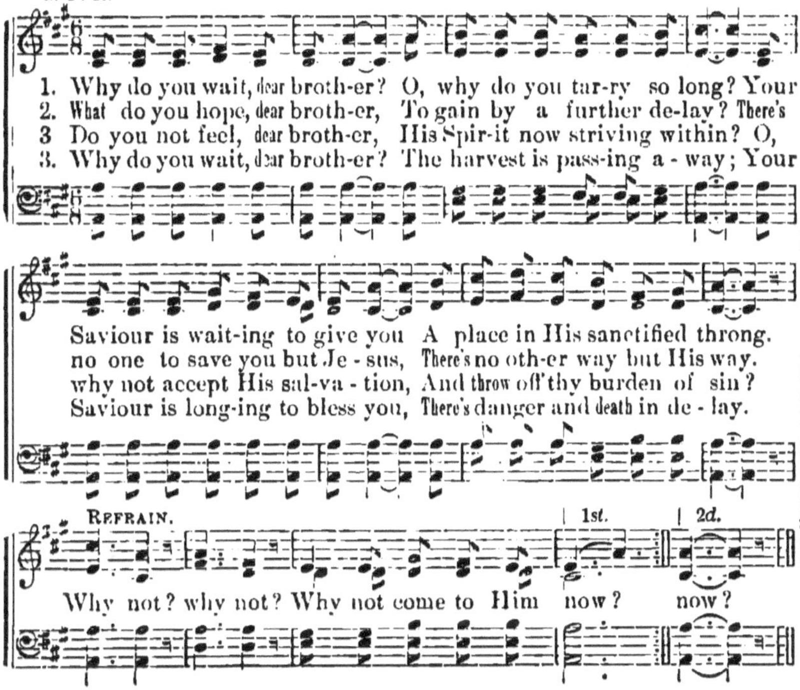

1. Why do you wait, dear broth-er? O, why do you tar-ry so long? Your
2. What do you hope, dear broth-er, To gain by a further de-lay? There's
3. Do you not feel, dear broth-er, His Spir-it now striving within? O,
3. Why do you wait, dear broth-er? The harvest is pass-ing a-way; Your

Saviour is wait-ing to give you A place in His sanctified throng.
no one to save you but Je-sus, There's no oth-er way but His way.
why not accept His sal-va-tion, And throw off thy burden of sin?
Saviour is long-ing to bless you, There's danger and death in de-lay.

REFRAIN.

Why not? why not? Why not come to Him now? now?

No. 137. Come, Come to Jesus.

"Come unto me."—Matt. 11: 28.

George B. Peck.
Hubert P. Main, by per.

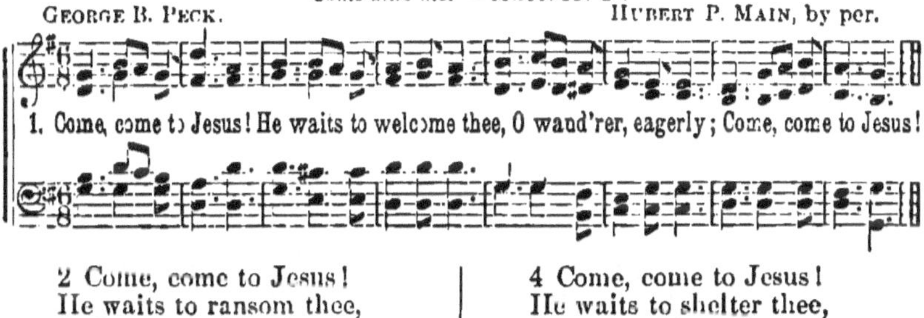

1. Come, come to Jesus! He waits to welcome thee, O wand'rer, eagerly; Come, come to Jesus!

2 Come, come to Jesus!
He waits to ransom thee,
O slave, so willingly;
Come, come to Jesus!

3 Come, come to Jesus!
He waits to lighten thee,
O burdened, graciously;
Come, come to Jesus!

4 Come, come to Jesus!
He waits to shelter thee,
O weary, blessedly;
Come, come to Jesus!

5 Come, come to Jesus!
He waits to carry thee,
O soul, so lovingly;
Come, come to Jesus!

No. 138. Jesus is my Saviour.

"— went on his way rejoicing." — ACTS 8: 39.

R. L.
ROBERT LOWRY.

1. My soul is hap-py all day long—Je-sus is my Sav-iour;
2. My heav-y load of sin is gone—Je-sus is my Sav-iour;
3. I heard the voice of mer-cy call—Je-sus is my Sav-iour;
4. Now will I tell it all a-round—Je-sus is my Sav-iour;

And all my life is full of song—Je-sus died for me.
At His dear cross I laid it down—Je-sus died for me.
I sim-ply trust-ed, that was all— Je-sus died for me.
How sweet a bless-ing I have found—Je-sus died for me.

Copyright, 1868, by ROBERT LOWRY.

REFRAIN.

Hal-le-lu-jah, hal-le-lu-jah To the lov-ing Lamb for sin-ners slain! Hal-le-lu-jah, hal-le-lu-jah To the Lamb who lives again!

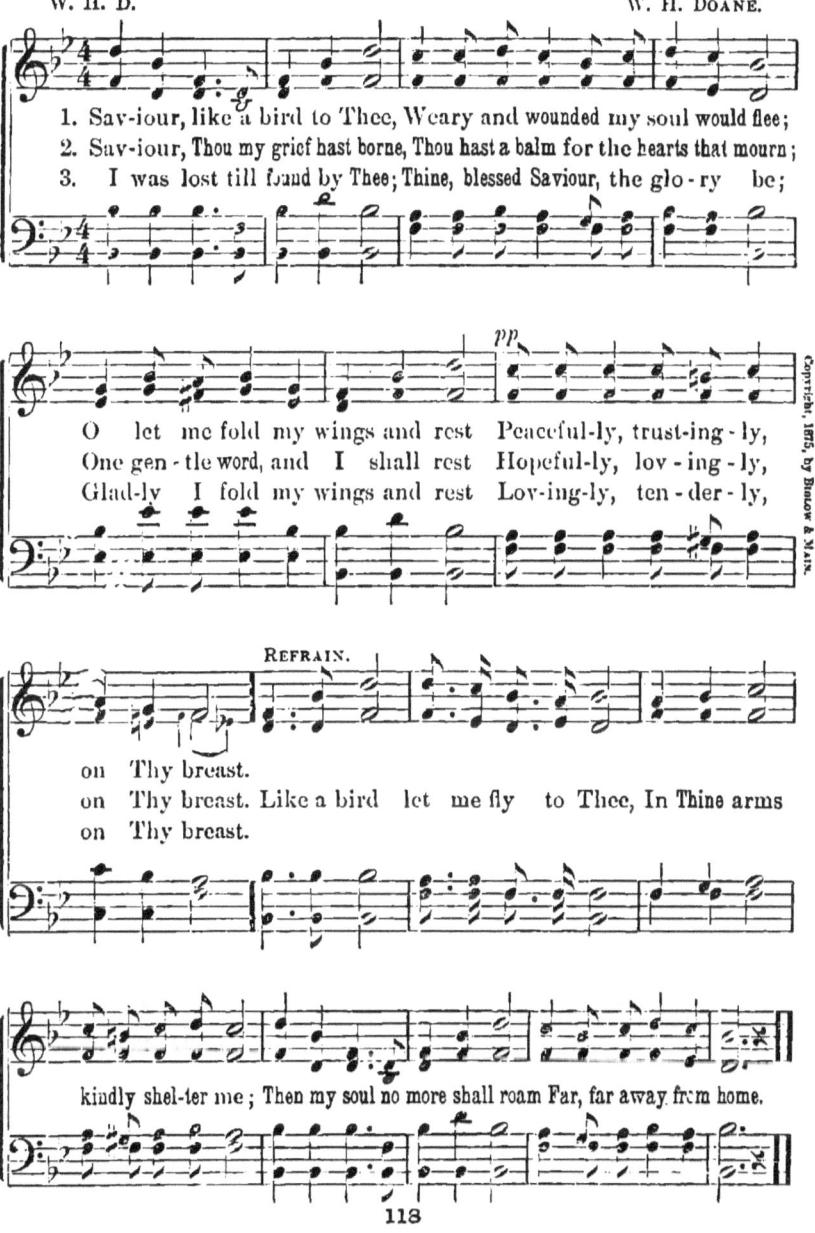

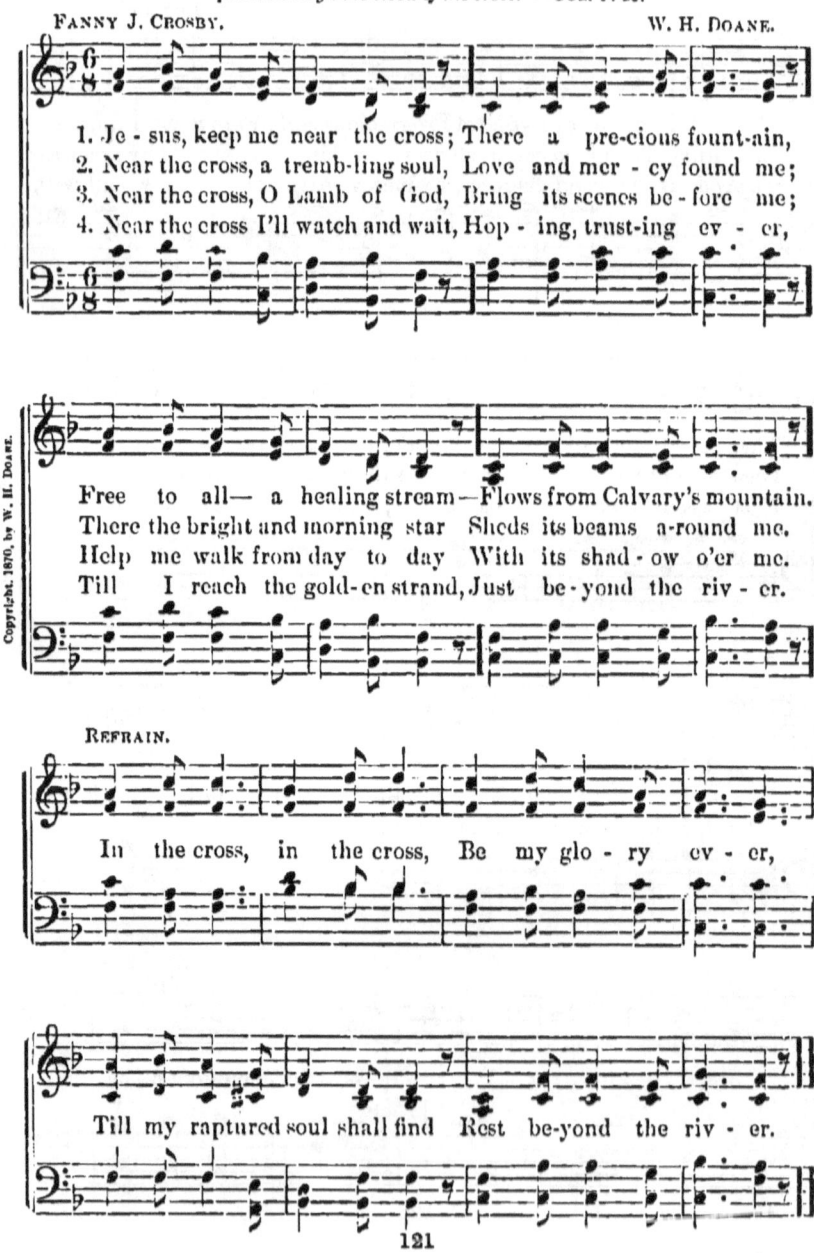

No. 144. I am Saved.

"According to his mercy he saved us."—TIT. 3: 5.

Mrs. ANNIE S. HAWKS.   ROBERT LOWRY.

1. I am saved! I am saved! Je-sus bids me go free;
2. Wondrous love! wondrous love! Now the gift I re-ceive;
3. I was weak— I am strong In the pow'r of His might;
4. Praise the Lord! praise the Lord! Ye His saints ev-'ry-where;

He has bought with a price E-ven me, e-ven me.
I have rest in His word, I be-lieve, I be-lieve.
And my dark-ness He turns In-to light, in-to light.
I shall join in the throng O-ver there, o-ver there.

Copyright, 1877, by R. Lowry.

REFRAIN.

Hal-le-lu-jah, Hal-le-lu-jah! Hal-le-lu-jah to my Sav-iour;

Hal-le-lu-jah, Hal-le-lu-jah, Hal-le-lu-jah, A-men.

No. 145. Tell it With Joy.

"My brethren, rejoice in the Lord."—PHIL. 3: 1.

Mrs. F. J. VAN ALSTYNE.   W. H. DOANE.

1. Tell it with joy, tell it with joy, Love in my bosom is glowing;
Jesus' blood has cleansed me, Jesus has made me free; Tell it again,
tell it again; O the sweet rapture of pardon; Grace divine has saved me,
And Jesus my all shall be. Weary and lonely, Seeking in vain for
pleasure, Far from the fold my spirit had gone astray;

D. S. Tell it again, tell it again; etc.

2 Tell it with joy, tell it with joy;
Wonderful, wonderful story!
I was lost till mercy
Sweetly came down from heaven;
Tell it with joy, tell it with joy;
Now I am happy in Jesus;
All is calm and peaceful,
And all of my sins forgiven.
I will adore Him,
Jesus, my dear Redeemer;
Yes, I will give Him glory from day
to day.—*Tell it again*, etc.

3 Come unto Him, come unto Him;
Mercy is tenderly pleading;
Weary, heavy laden,
Still there is room for thee:
Only believe, only believe;
Jesus is ready and willing;
All may come and welcome,
Salvation for all is free.
Why will ye linger?
Mercy is still entreating;
Come and be happy, come and with
rapture say:—*Tell it again*, etc.

No. 146. He Comes to Save.

"Behold the Lamb of God, which taketh away the sin of the world." — JOHN 1:29.

REV. W. T. SLEEPER.   D. B. TOWNER, by per.

1. Behold the Lamb of God, He comes to save;
   Behold His flowing blood, He comes to save;
   D.C. Jesus is passing by, He comes to save.

2. Ye fearful souls, draw near, He comes to save;
   Ye dying sinners, hear, He comes to save;
   D.C. And counting not the cost, He comes to save.

   Ye who for healing sigh, Ye who for mercy cry,
   He comes to save the lost, On raging billows tossed,

3 He comes thy love to win, He comes to save;
He comes to conquer sin, He comes to save;
He comes to crush thy foe, The path of life to show,
And rescue thee from woe; He comes to save.

No. 147. Happy Day.

"Whoso trusteth in the LORD, happy is he." — PROV. 16:20.

PHILIP DODDRIDGE, D. D.   E. F. RIMBAULT.

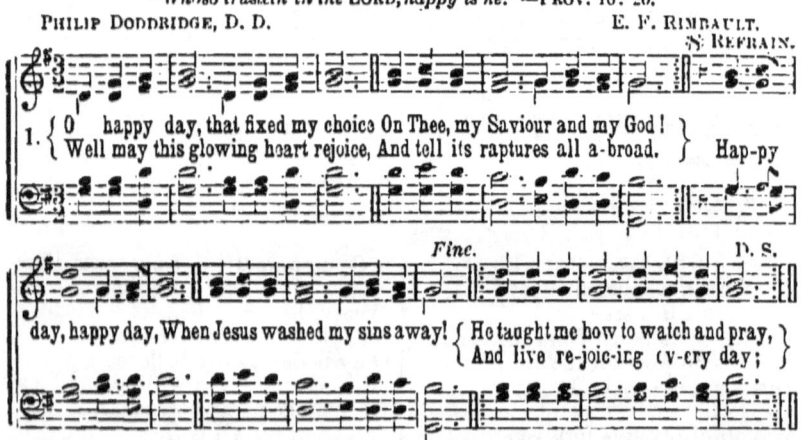

1. O happy day, that fixed my choice On Thee, my Saviour and my God!
   Well may this glowing heart rejoice, And tell its raptures all abroad. Happy day, happy day, When Jesus washed my sins away! He taught me how to watch and pray, And live rejoicing every day;

2 'Tis done,—the great transaction's done;
I am my Lord's and He is mine;
He drew me, and I followed on,
Rejoiced to own the call divine.

3 Now rest, my long-divided heart,
Fixed on this blissful center, rest;
Here have I found a nobler part,
Here heavenly pleasures fill my breast.

No. 148. Saved by the Blood.

"The blood . . . cleanseth us from all sin." —1 JOHN 1: 7.

FANNY J. CROSBY.   W. H. DOANE.

1. We're saved by the blood That was drawn from the side Of Je - sus our
2. O yes, 'tis the blood Of the Lamb that was slain; He conquered the
3. We're saved by the blood, We are sealed by its power; 'Tis life to the
4. We're saved by the blood, Hal-le - lu - jah a - gain; We're saved by the

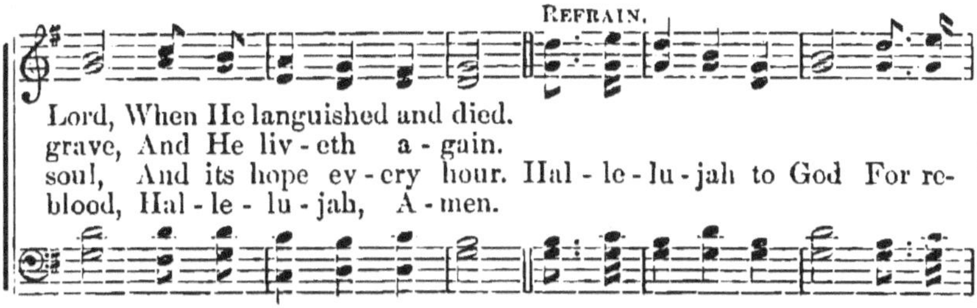

REFRAIN.

Lord, When He languished and died.
grave, And He liv - eth a - gain.
soul, And its hope ev - ery hour. Hal - le - lu - jah to God For re-
blood, Hal - le - lu - jah, A - men.

demption so free! Hal-le-lu-jah, Halle-lu-jah, Dear Saviour, to Thee.

No. 149. Child of Sin and Sorrow.

"Incline your ear, and come unto me." —ISA. 55: 3.

THOMAS HASTINGS.   DR. THOMAS HASTINGS.

1. { Child of sin and sorrow, Filled with dismay, }
  { Wait not for to-mor-row, Yield thee to - day; } Heav'n bids thee come While yet there's room;
D. C. Child of sin and sorrow, Hear and o - bey.

2 Child of sin and sorrow,
Why wilt thou die?
Come while thou canst borrow
Help from on high;

Grieve not that love
Which from above,
Child of sin and sorrow,
Would bring thee nigh.

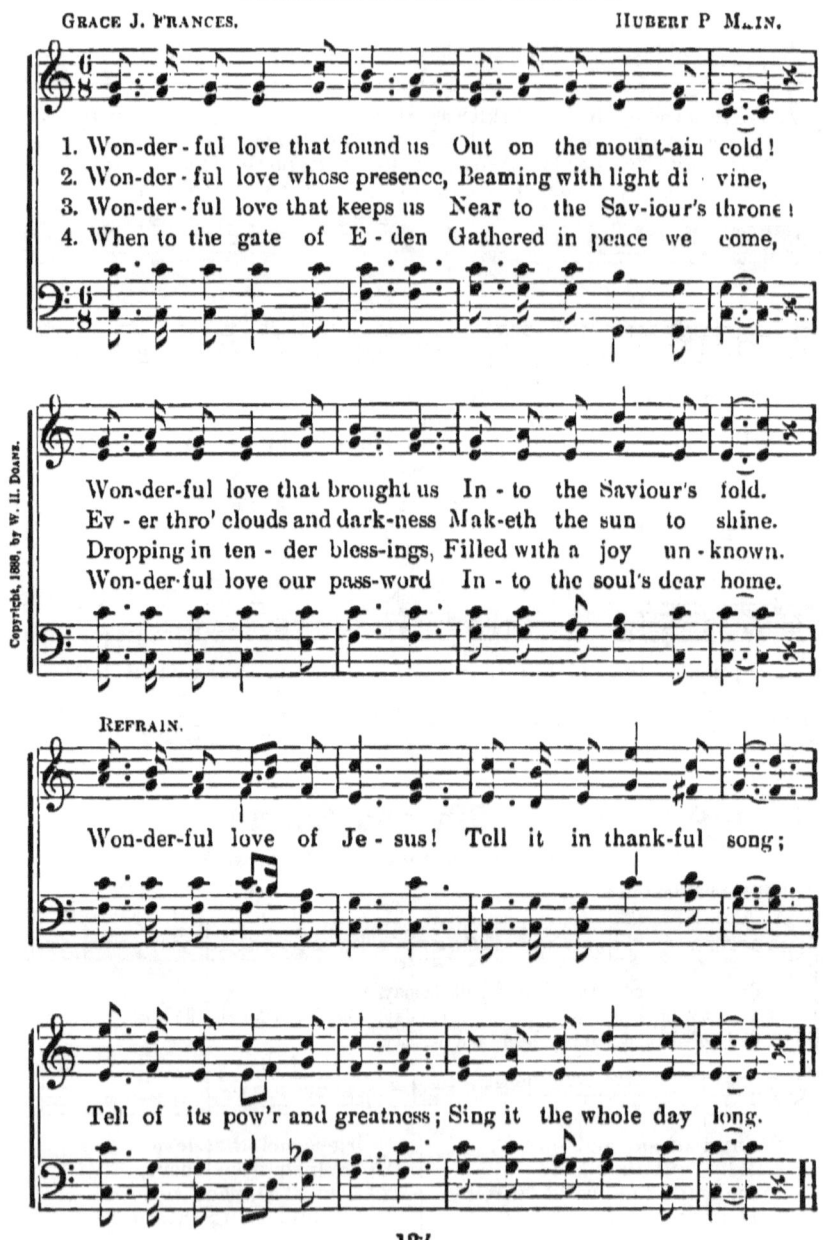

No. 151. Father, Lead Thou Me.

"He leadeth me."—Ps. 23: 2.

HELEN R. YOUNG. ROBERT LOWRY.

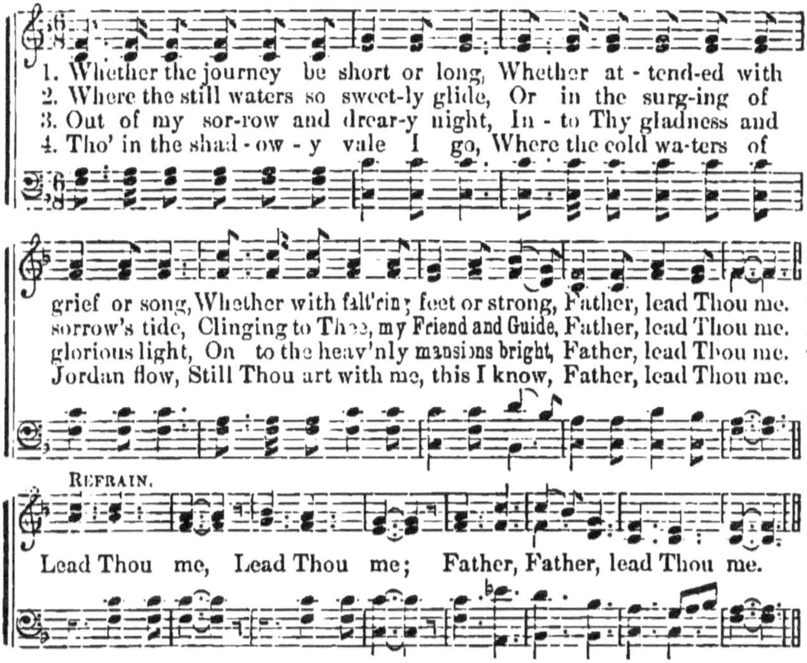

1. Whether the journey be short or long, Whether at-tend-ed with
2. Where the still waters so sweet-ly glide, Or in the surg-ing of
3. Out of my sor-row and drear-y night, In - to Thy gladness and
4. Tho' in the shad - ow - y vale I go, Where the cold wa-ters of

grief or song, Whether with fall'ring feet or strong, Father, lead Thou me.
sorrow's tide, Clinging to Thee, my Friend and Guide, Father, lead Thou me.
glorious light, On to the heav'nly mansions bright, Father, lead Thou me.
Jordan flow, Still Thou art with me, this I know, Father, lead Thou me.

Copyright, 1884, by Robert Lowry.

REFRAIN.

Lead Thou me, Lead Thou me; Father, Father, lead Thou me.

No. 152. There is a Fountain.

"Peace through the blood of his cross."—COL. 1: 20.

WILLIAM COWPER. Western Melody.

1. { There is a fountain filled with blood Drawn from Immanuel's veins;
   And sinners plunged beneath that flood, (*Omit.*) . . Lose all their guilty stains.

D. C. And sinners plunged beneath that flood (*Omit.*) . . Lose all their guilty stains.

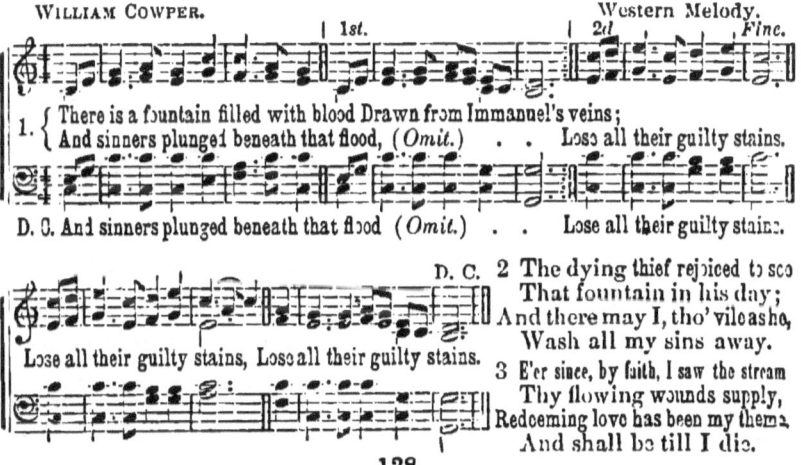

Lose all their guilty stains, Lose all their guilty stains.

D. C. 2 The dying thief rejoiced to see
That fountain in his day;
And there may I, tho' vile as he,
Wash all my sins away.

3 E'er since, by faith, I saw the stream
Thy flowing wounds supply,
Redeeming love has been my theme,
And shall be till I die.

No. 156. Solid Rock.

"Thou art my rock and my fortress."—Ps. 31: 3.

Rev. Edward Mote.   Wm. B. Bradbury, by per.

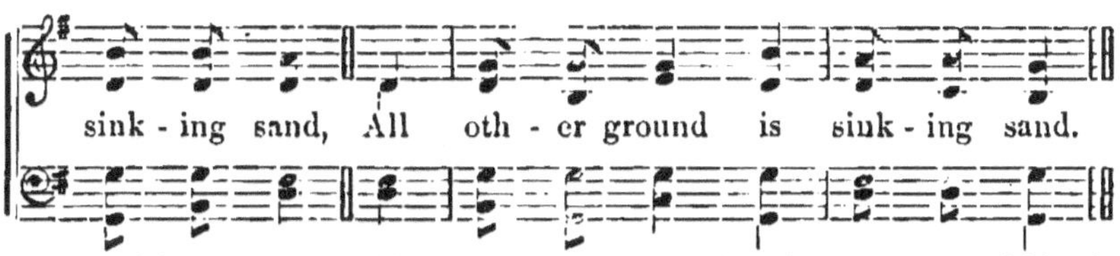

1. My hope is built on nothing less Than Jesus' blood and righteousness;
I dare not trust the sweetest frame, But wholly lean on Jesus' name;
On Christ, the solid rock, I stand; All other ground is sinking sand, All other ground is sinking sand.

2 When darkness seems to veil His face,
I rest on His unchanging grace;
In every high and stormy gale,
My anchor holds within the vail;
On Christ, the solid rock, I stand;
All other ground is sinking sand.

3 His oath, His covenant and blood,
Support me in the whelming flood;
When all around my soul gives way,
He then is all my hope and stay;
On Christ, the solid rock, I stand;
All other ground is sinking sand.

No. 157. Coronation.

"Let us exalt his name together."—Ps. 34: 3.

Rev. Edward Perronet.   Oliver Holden.

1. All hail the pow'r of Jesus' name, Let angels prostrate fall;
Bring forth the royal diadem, And crown Him Lord of all;

Coronation. Concluded.

2 Ye chosen seed of Israel's race,
    A remnant weak and small,
Hail Him who saves you by His grace,
    And crown Him Lord of all.

3 Let every kindred, every tribe,
    On this terrestrial ball,

To Him all majesty ascribe,
    And crown Him Lord of all.

4 O that with yonder sacred throng,
    We at His feet may fall;
We'll join the everlasting song,
    And crown Him Lord of all.

No. 158. Hide Thou Me.

"Thou art my hiding place."—Ps. 32: 7.

FANNY J. CROSBY. ROBERT LOWRY.

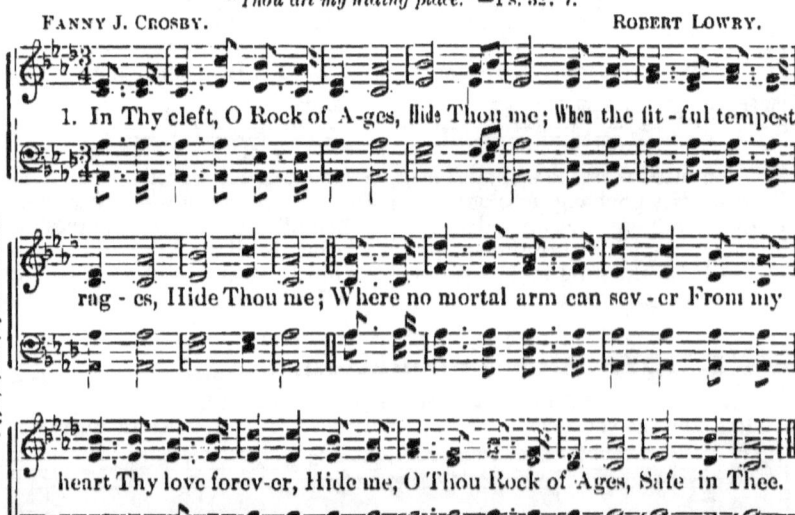

2 From the snare of sinful pleasure,
    Hide Thou me;
Thou, my soul's eternal treasure,
    Hide Thou me;
When the world its power is wielding,
And my heart is almost yielding,
Hide me, O Thou Rock of Ages,
    Safe in Thee.

3 In the lonely night of sorrow,
    Hide Thou me;
Till in glory dawns the morrow,
    Hide Thou me;
In the sight of Jordan's billow,
Let Thy bosom be my pillow;
Hide me, O Thou Rock of Ages,
    Safe in Thee.

No. 160. Hold Thou Me Up.

"Jesus stretched forth his hand, and caught him." —MATT. 14: 31.

FANNY J. CROSBY.   W. H. DOANE.

1. O Saviour mine, who now beholdest me, 'Tis heav'n below Thy love to know; My feet with joyful haste would follow Thee; Lead Thou me on wher-e'er I go.
2. O Saviour mine, whose wings o'ershadow me, No friend so near, no name so dear; Thou art my hope of immortality, Thy voice alone my heart can cheer.
3. O Saviour mine, how great Thy love to me! Its beams divine, how bright they shine! Hold Thou me up, let me abide in Thee; Keep Thou my hand still firm in Thine.
4. O Saviour mine, when thou shalt call for me Thy robe to wear, Thy joy to share, Though endless years my happy song shall be, Thy grace, Thy love, that brought me there.

REFRAIN.

Hold Thou me up, lead Thou me on, My guide, my stay, o'er life's dark way; Hold Thou me up, lead Thou me on, Shall be my pray'r from day to day.

Copyright, 1884, by Biglow & Main.

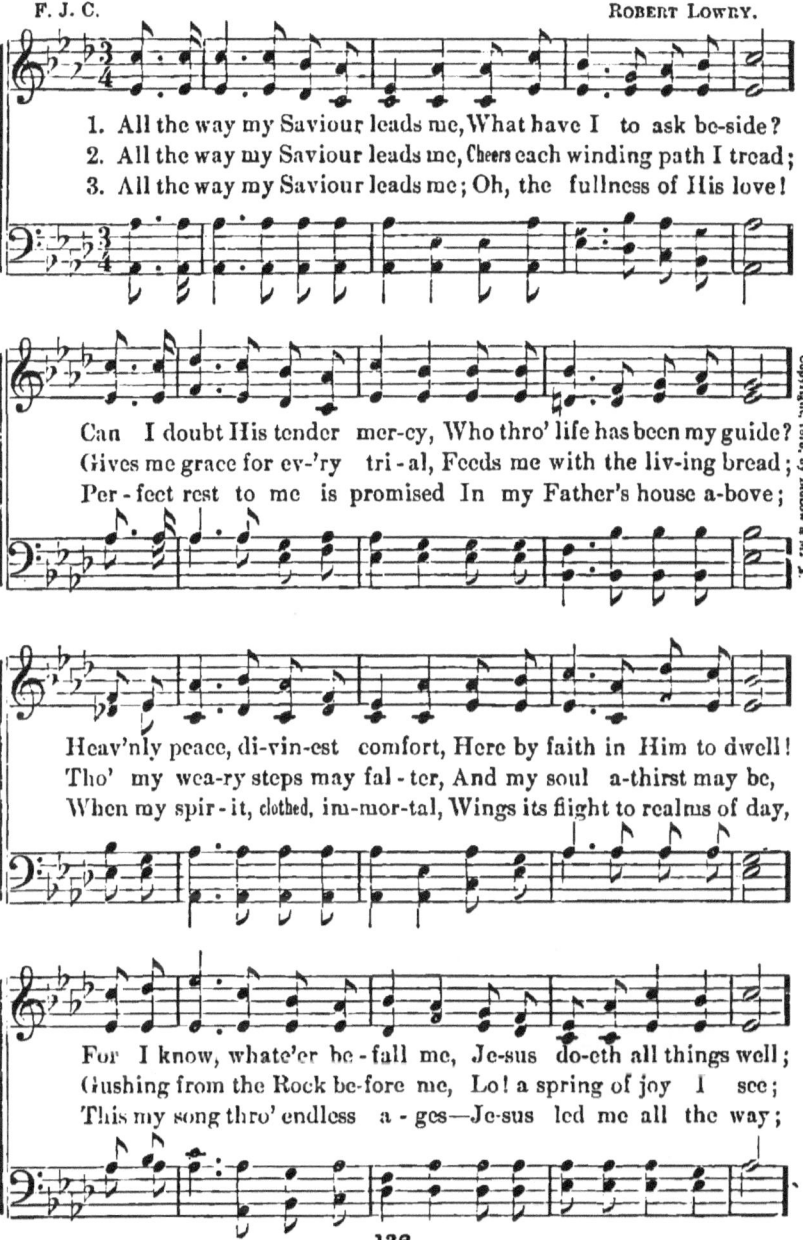

No. 165. Precious Promise.

"Whereby are given unto us exceeding great and precious promises." —2 Pet. 1: 4.

NATHANIEL NILES.   P. P. BLISS.

1. Pre-cious promise God hath given To the wea-ry pass-er by,
2. When temptations al-most win thee, And thy trusted watchers fly,
3. When thy se-cret hopes have perished In the grave of years gone by,
4. When the shades of life are fall-ing, And the hour has come to die,

On the way from earth to heav-en, "I will guide thee with Mine eye."
Let this prom-ise ring with-in thee, "I will guide thee with Mine eye."
Let this prom-ise still be cherished, "I will guide thee with Mine eye."
Hear thy trust-y Pi-lot call-ing, "I will guide thee with Mine eye."

By per. of The John Church Co., owners of copyright.

REFRAIN.

I will guide thee, I will guide thee, I will guide thee with Mine eye;

On the way from earth to heav-en I will guide thee with Mine eye.

No. 166. Thou Hast Redeemed Me.

"*I have redeemed thee.*" Isa. 43:1.

FANNY J. CROSBY.   W. H. DOANE.

1. O-ver my spir-it, si-lent-ly mus-ing, Came a sweet mes-sage, peaceful, di-vine; Glad-ly I heard it, slowly re-peat-ing, I have redeem'd thee and thou art mine.
2. Rich are the bless-ings Thou art be-stow-ing, Boun-ti-ful Shepherd, Sav-iour di-vine; I shall not wea-ry, walking be-side Thee, Thou hast redeem'd me, my life is Thine. Thou hast re-
3. Green are the past-ures, cool are the wa-ters, Where at the noon-tide oft I re-cline; How shall I thank Thee, how shall I praise Thee? Thou hast redeem'd me, my life is Thine.

REFRAIN.—Ten-der-ly fold me, lov-ing-ly hold me; Hid-ing for-ev-er my soul in Thee.

D. S. REFRAIN.—deem'd me, wonderful Saviour, Under Thy watch-care still would I be;

No. 167. Only One Name.

"The name of Jesus." —PHIL. 2: 10.

REV. ROBERT LOWRY.   W. H. DOANE.

1. There is only one Name that the saints adore—Jesus, our Elder
2. There is only one Name that the soul need know—Jesus, the Lord's A-
3. There is only one Name that the an-gels sing—Jesus, the Lord of

Broth-er; They give Him all the praise, now and evermore; His
noint-ed; He suf-fered to re-deem us from sin and woe, And
Glo-ry; They gather at His feet while they hail Him King, And

REFRAIN.

Name is o-ver ev-ery oth-er.
bear us to the rest ap-point-ed.   Then lift the happy strain, And
list-en to Redemption's story.

sing the glad refrain—The Name, the Name of Je-sus; Je-sus.

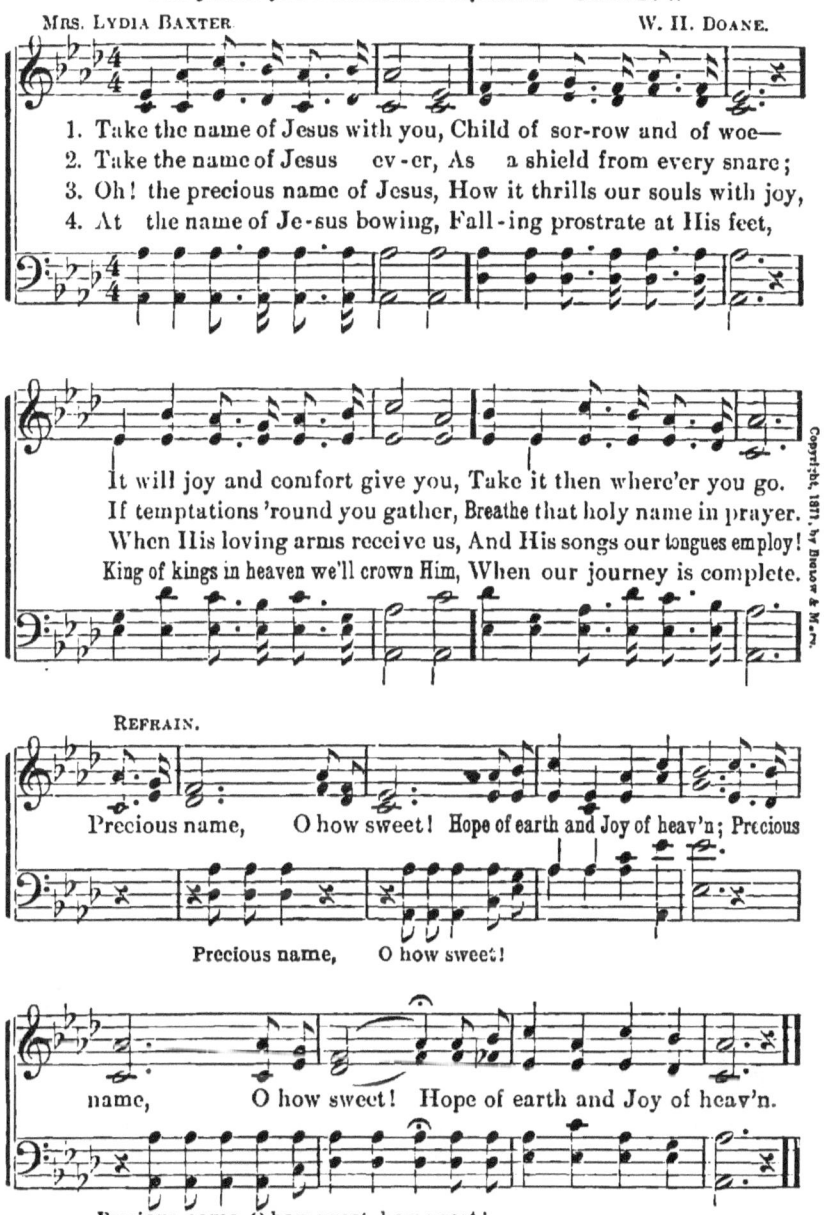

No. 170. The Name I Love.

"I will bless thy name forever."—Ps. 145: 1.

REV. FREDERICK WHITFIELD.   W. H. DOANE.

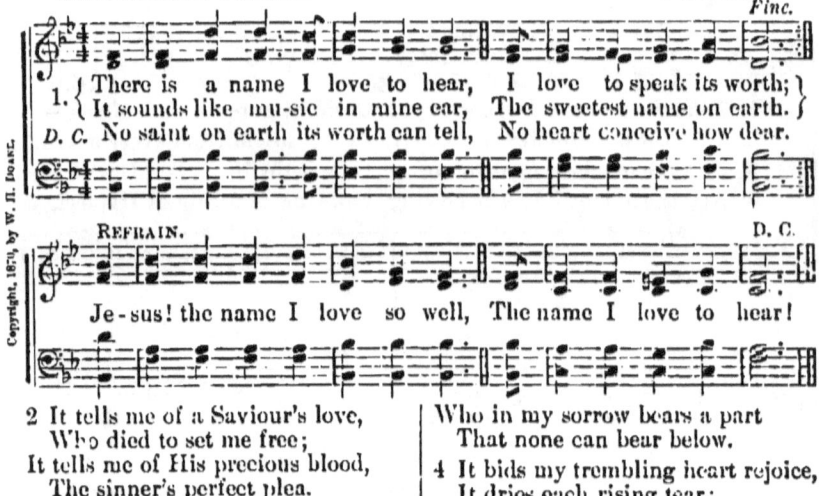

2 It tells me of a Saviour's love,
Who died to set me free;
It tells me of His precious blood,
The sinner's perfect plea.
3. It tells of One whose loving heart
Can feel my deepest woe,

Who in my sorrow bears a part
That none can bear below.
4 It bids my trembling heart rejoice,
It dries each rising tear;
It tells me, in a "still, small voice,"
To trust, and never fear.

No. 171. No Name so Sweet.

"Thou shalt call his name Jesus." MATT. 1: 21.

REV. GEORGE W. BETHUNE.   W. B. BRADBURY, by per.

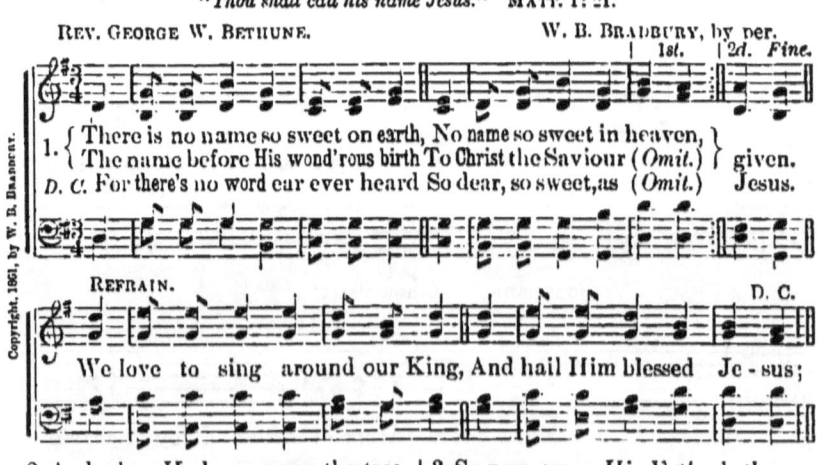

2 And when He hung upon the tree,
They wrote this name above Him,
That all might see the reason we
For evermore must love Him.

3 So now, upon His Father's throne,
Almighty to release us
From sin and pains, He ever reigns,
The Prince and Saviour, Jesus.

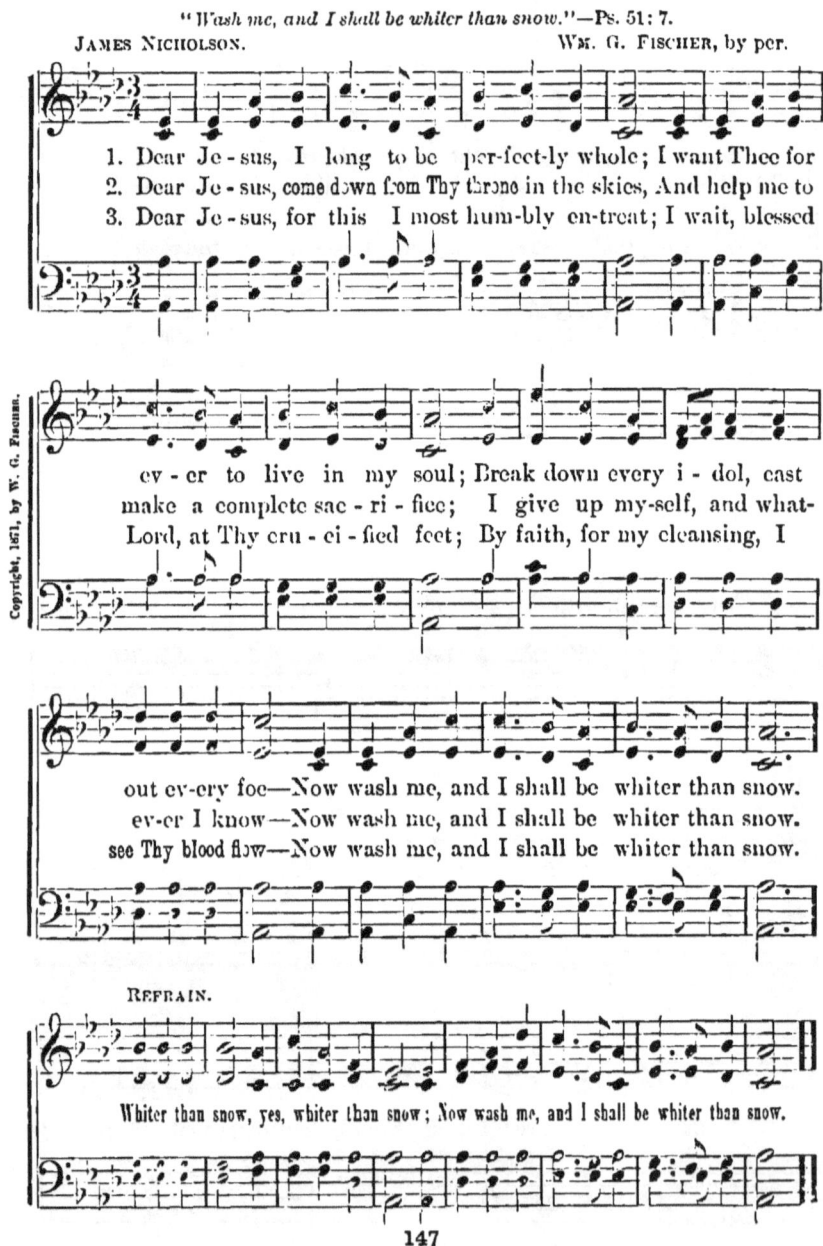

No. 176. Longing for Christ.

"The very God of peace sanctify you wholly." —1 Thess. 5: 23.

C. W. Ray, D. D.
Robert Lowry.

1. My heart is sad and wea-ry, My way is dark and drear-y;
2. My sky is o-ver-cloud-ed, My path with shadows shrouded;
3. From sin Thou canst de-liv-er, And break its bonds for-ev-er;

O quench my cease-less long-ings With Thy rich grace and love;
Dis-pel the mock-ing phan-toms, And drive a-way the gloom;
O let me nev-er wan-der And grieve Thee, I im-plore;

With Thine own arm up-hold me, And to Thy breast en-fold me;
A balm for ev-'ry sor-row From Thee I fain would borrow;
Un-ho-ly thoughts subduing, My sin-ful heart re-new-ing,

O sanc-ti-fy me whol-ly, And bring me safe a-bove.
For Thee my soul is long-ing, And waits to make Thee room.
O guide me to Thy glo-ry, And bless me ev-er-more.

Copyright, 1889, by Robert Lowry.

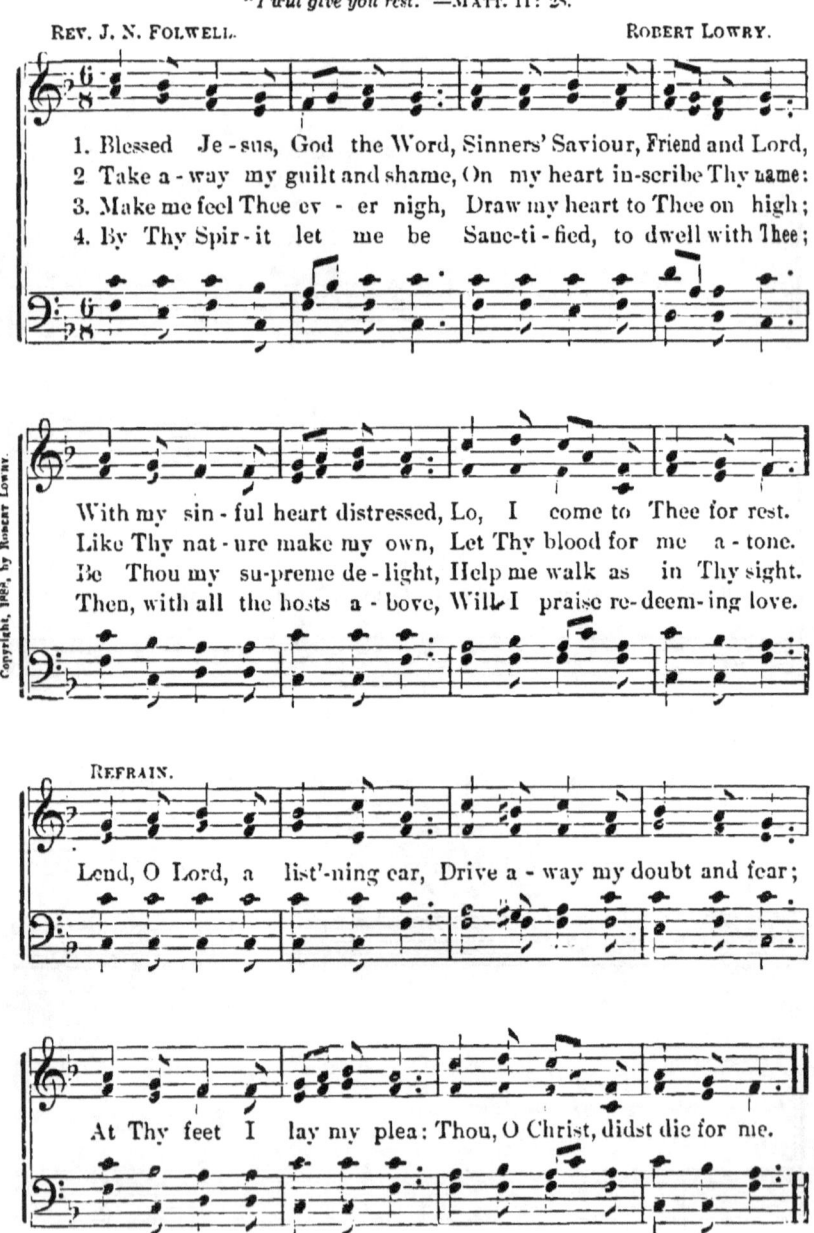

No. 180. Bringing in the Sheaves.

"*The harvest is the end of the world.*"—MATT. 13: 39.

KNOWLES SHAW.   GEO. A. MINOR, by per.

1. Sowing in the morning, sowing seeds of kind-ness, Sowing in the noontide
2. Sowing in the sunshine, sowing in the shadows, Fearing neither clouds nor
3. Go, then, ever weeping, sowing for the Master, 'Tho' the loss sustained our

and the dewy eves; Waiting for the harvest, and the time of reaping,
winter's chilling breeze; By and by the harvest, and the la-bor end-ed,
spir-it oft-en grieves: When our weeping's o-ver, He will bid us welcome,

REFRAIN.

We shall come re-joicing, bringing in the sheaves. Bringing in the sheaves,

bringing in the sheaves, We shall come re-joic-ing, bringing in the sheaves;

Bringing in the sheaves, bringing in the sheaves, We shall come rejoicing, bringing in the sheaves.

The Banner of the Cross. Concluded.

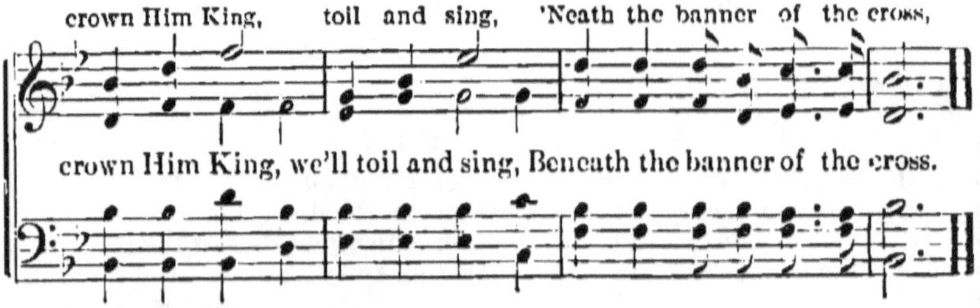
crown Him King, toil and sing, 'Neath the banner of the cross,
crown Him King, we'll toil and sing, Beneath the banner of the cross.

No. 183. Jesus, Saviour, Pilot Me.

"In him will I trust."—2 Sam. 22: 3.

Rev. Edward Hopper. J. E. Gould.

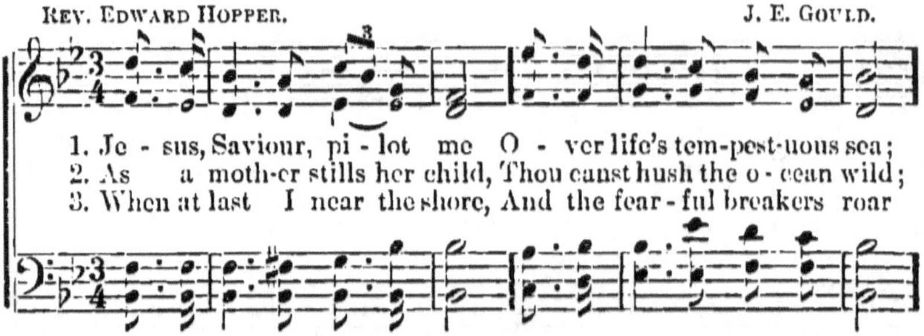
1. Je - sus, Saviour, pi - lot me O - ver life's tem-pest-uous sea;
2. As a moth-er stills her child, Thou canst hush the o - cean wild;
3. When at last I near the shore, And the fear - ful breakers roar

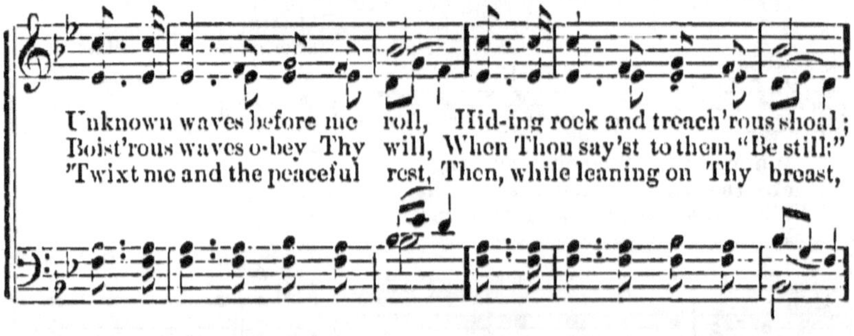
Unknown waves before me roll, Hid-ing rock and treach'rous shoal;
Boist'rous waves o-bey Thy will, When Thou say'st to them, "Be still;"
'Twixt me and the peaceful rest, Then, while leaning on Thy breast,

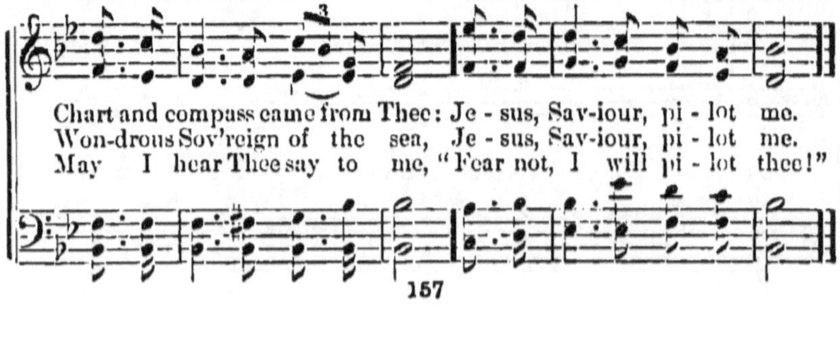
Chart and compass came from Thee: Je - sus, Sav-iour, pi - lot me.
Won-drous Sov'reign of the sea, Je - sus, Sav-iour, pi - lot me.
May I hear Thee say to me, "Fear not, I will pi - lot thee!"

No. 184. Path of Love.

"— and we will walk in his paths."—Isa. 2: 3.

Mrs. E. L. Park. W. H. Doane.

1. O my Saviour, may Thy Spir-it Be my constant faithful guide;
2. When temptations gather dark-ly, Hold my trembling hand in Thine;
3. Should I fal-ter on my journey, O my Sav-iour, comfort me;
4. Till my wea-ry march is ended, And the Cit-y gate I see,

Thro' the changing scenes be-fore me, Keep me walking near Thy side.
Keep me walk-ing in the brightness Of Thy blessed Light di-vine.
Keep me walk-ing firm-ly onward, On-ly trust-ing, Lord, in Thee.
Till I en-ter full of rapture, Keep me walking still with Thee.

Copyright, 1886, by W. H. Doane.

REFRAIN.

Keep me walk - ing, dai - ly walk - ing, Keep me
Keep me dai - ly walk-ing, Keep me dai - ly walk-ing,

walk-ing in the path of love; Keep me walk - ing, dai - ly
Keep me dai - ly walking, Keep me

walk - ing, Keep me walk-ing in the path of love.
walk-ing, walk-ing,

No. 186. The Half Can Never be Told.

"The half was not told me."—1 KINGS 10: 7.

FANNY J. CROSBY. W. H. DOANE.

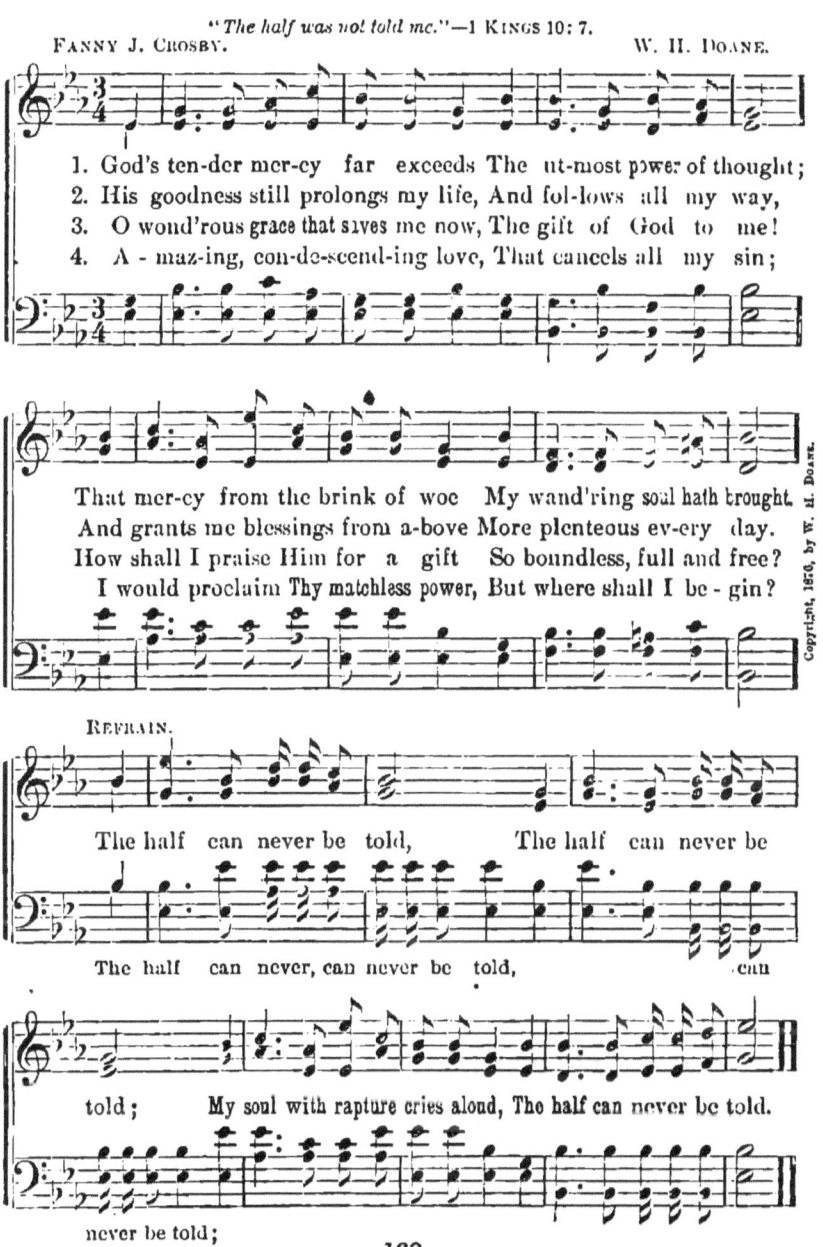

1. God's ten-der mer-cy far exceeds The ut-most power of thought;
2. His goodness still prolongs my life, And fol-lows all my way,
3. O wond'rous grace that saves me now, The gift of God to me!
4. A-maz-ing, con-de-scend-ing love, That cancels all my sin;

That mer-cy from the brink of woe My wand'ring soul hath brought.
And grants me blessings from a-bove More plenteous ev-ery day.
How shall I praise Him for a gift So boundless, full and free?
I would proclaim Thy matchless power, But where shall I be-gin?

REFRAIN.

The half can never be told, The half can never be told;
The half can never, can never be told, can
My soul with rapture cries aloud, The half can never be told.
never be told;

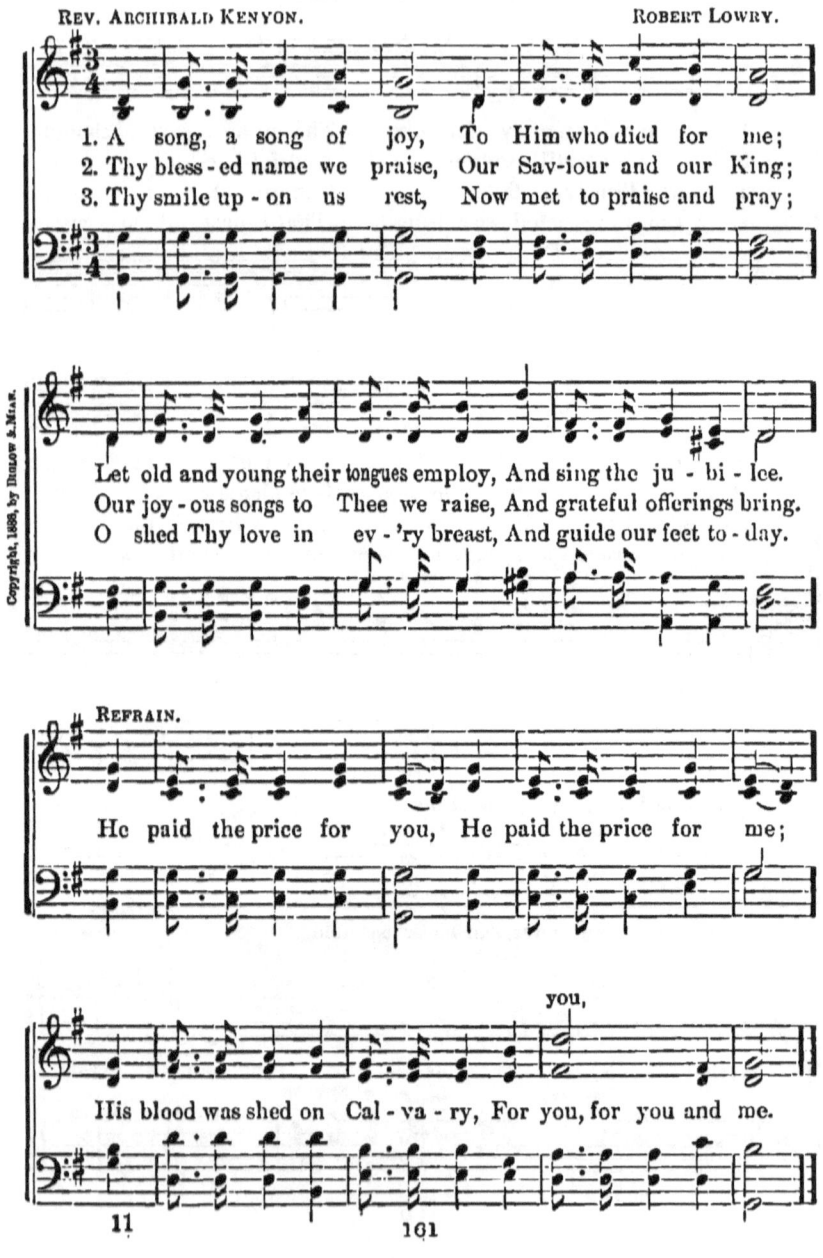

No. 189. O Thou Lamb of Calvary!

"It is finished."—JOHN 19: 30.

R. L.
Tenderly.
ROBERT LOWRY.

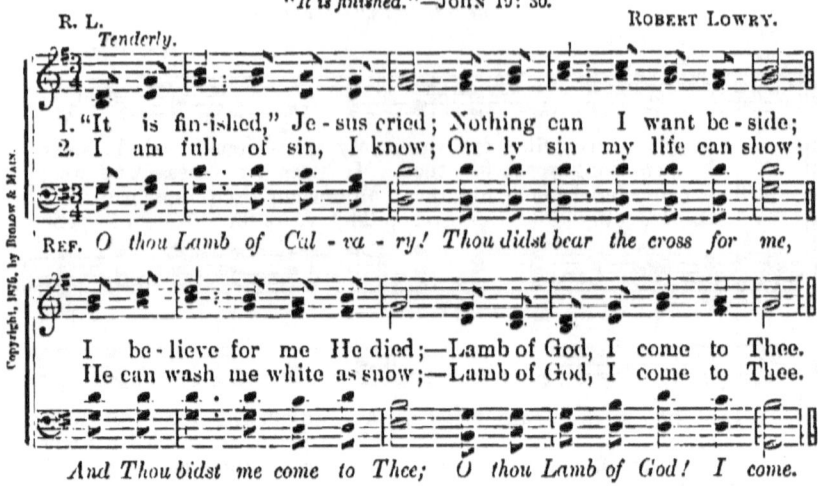

1. "It is fin-ished," Je-sus cried; Nothing can I want be-side;
2. I am full of sin, I know; On-ly sin my life can show;

REF. O thou Lamb of Cal-va-ry! Thou didst bear the cross for me,

I be-lieve for me He died;—Lamb of God, I come to Thee.
He can wash me white as snow;—Lamb of God, I come to Thee.

And Thou bidst me come to Thee; O thou Lamb of God! I come.

3 Poor and needy though I be,
There is wealth in Christ for me;
There is grace to make me free;—
Lamb of God, I come to Thee.—

4 Jesus knows my every need;
Jesus is a friend indeed;
Now I hear Him intercede;—
Lamb of God, I come to Thee.

No. 190. Alas! and did My Saviour Bleed?

"—Christ died for our sins."—1 COR. 15: 3.

ISAAC WATTS.
W. H. DOANE.

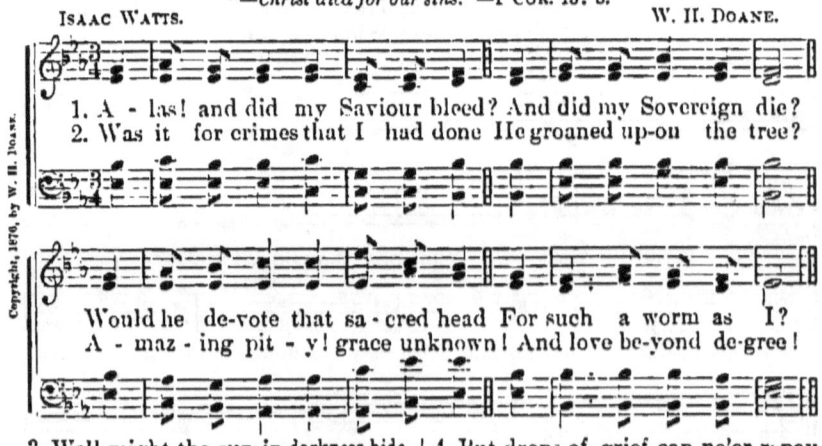

1. A-las! and did my Saviour bleed? And did my Sovereign die?
2. Was it for crimes that I had done He groaned up-on the tree?

Would he de-vote that sa-cred head For such a worm as I?
A-maz-ing pit-y! grace unknown! And love be-yond de-gree!

3 Well might the sun in darkness hide,
And shut his glories in,
When Christ, the mighty Maker, died
For man the creature's sin.

4 But drops of grief can ne'er repay
The debt of love I owe;
Here, Lord, I give myself away,
'Tis all that I can do.

No. 191. Bread of Life.

"I am the bread of life." —JOHN 6: 35.

MARY A. LATHBURY. WM. F. SHERWIN, by per.

1. Break Thou the bread of life, dear Lord, to me, As Thou didst break the loaves be-side the sea; Be-yond the sa-cred page I seek Thee, Lord; My spir-it pants for Thee, O liv-ing Word!
2. Bless Thou the pre-cious truth, dear Lord, to me, As Thou didst bless the bread by Gal-i-lee; Then shall all bond-age cease, all fet-ters fall, And I shall find my peace, my all in all!

Copyright, 1877, by J. H. Vincent.

No. 192. Word Divine.

"The word of God is not bound." —2 TIM. 2: 9.

Tr. CATHERINE WINKWORTH. ROBERT LOWRY.

1. Spread, O spread, thou might-y word, Spread the kingdom of the Lord,
2. Word of life, most pure and strong, Lo, for thee the na-tions long;
3. Lord of har-vest, let there be Joy and strength to work for Thee;

Copyright, 1880, by Biglow & Main.

164

Word Divine. Concluded.

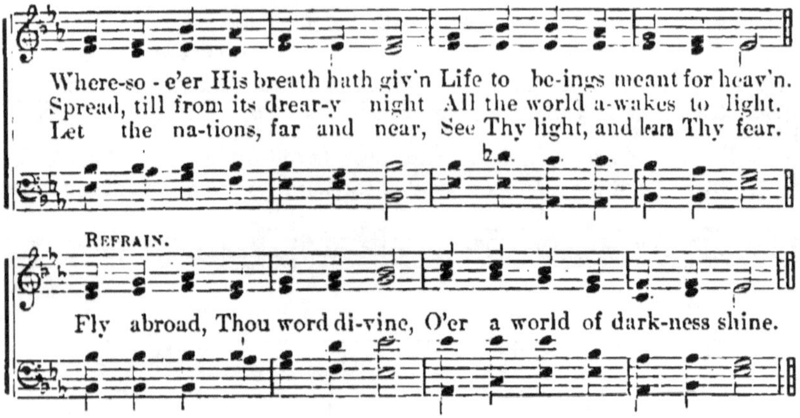

Where-so-e'er His breath hath giv'n Life to be-ings meant for heav'n.
Spread, till from its drear-y night All the world a-wakes to light.
Let the na-tions, far and near, See Thy light, and learn Thy fear.

REFRAIN.

Fly abroad, Thou word di-vine, O'er a world of dark-ness shine.

No. 193. How Much I Owe.

"I forgave thee all that debt."—MATT. 18: 32.

REV. R. M. MCCHEYNE.   ROBERT LOWRY.

1. When this pass-ing world is done, When has sunk life's set-ting
2. When I stand be-fore the throne, Dressed in beau-ty not my
3. When the praise of heav'n I hear, Break-ing on my raptured

sun; When I stand with Thee at last, Look-ing o'er my jour-ney
own; When I see Thee as Thou art, Love Thee with a per-fect
ear; When I join the ho-ly throng, Shar-ing in the hap-py

past— Lord, I then shall ful-ly know, Not till then, how much I owe.
heart—Lord, I then shall ful-ly know, Not till then, how much I owe.
song —Lord, I then shall ful-ly know, Not till then, how much I owe.

Copyright, 1886, by ROBERT LOWRY.

I Would Be a Light. Concluded.

I would be a light for Jesus, Shining night and day.

No. 195. Grant Us Thy Peace.

"Peace shall be upon Israel." — Ps. 125: 5

HENRY F. CHORLEY.   ROBERT LOWRY.
Moderato. 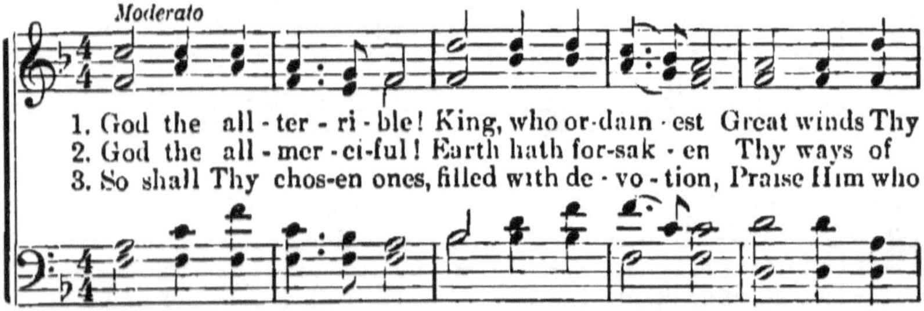

Copyright, 1893, by Robert Lowry.

1. God the all-ter-ri-ble! King, who or-dain-est Great winds Thy
2. God the all-mer-ci-ful! Earth hath for-sak-en Thy ways of
3. So shall Thy chos-en ones, filled with de-vo-tion, Praise Him who

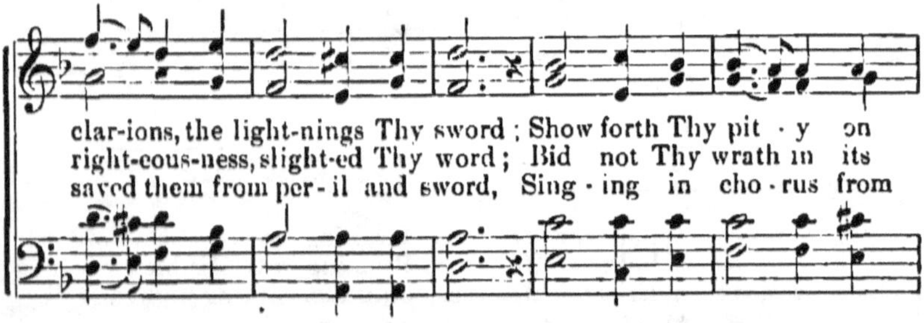

clar-ions, the light-nings Thy sword; Show forth Thy pit-y on
right-eous-ness, slight-ed Thy word; Bid not Thy wrath in its
saved them from per-il and sword, Sing-ing in cho-rus from

high where Thou reignest; Grant us Thy peace, O most merciful Lord.
ter-rors a-wak-en; Grant us Thy peace, O most mer-ci-ful Lord.
o-cean to o-cean, Sweet is the peace from our mer-ci-ful Lord.

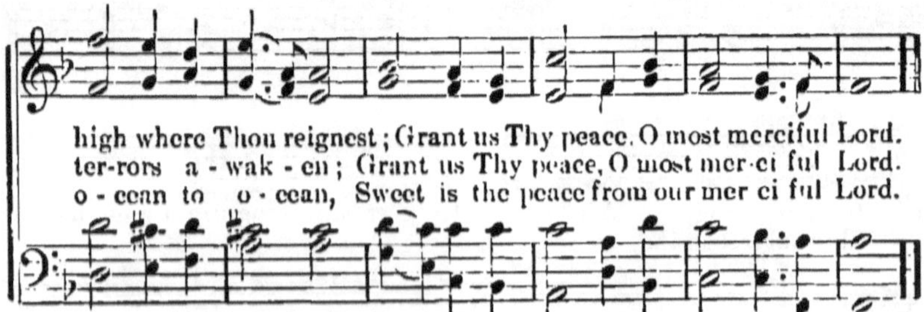

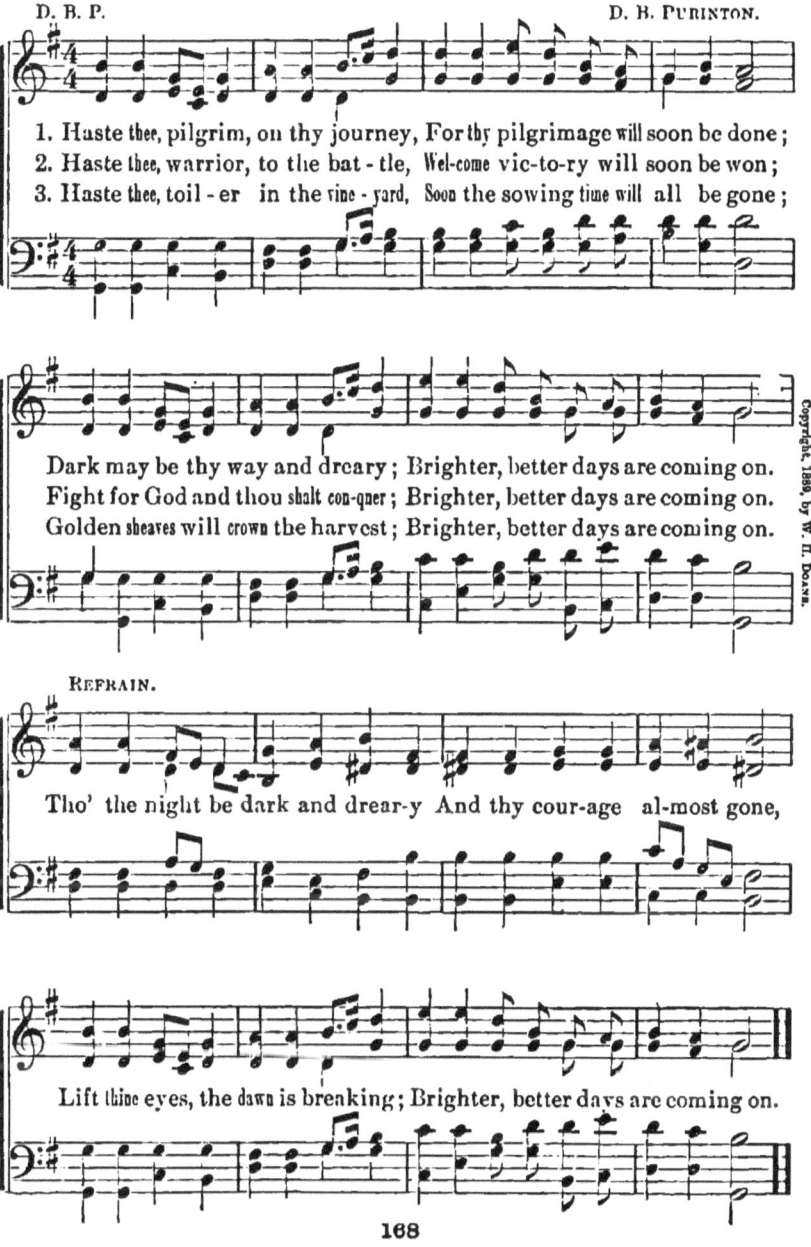

No. 198. Marching to Zion.

"Arise ye, and let us go up to Zion."—JER. 31: 6.

ISAAC WATTS. ROBERT LOWRY.

1. Come, ye that love the Lord, And let your joys be known, Join in a song with sweet ac-cord, Join in a song with sweet ac-cord, And thus sur-round the throne, And thus surround the throne.
2. Let those re-fuse to sing Who nev-er knew our God; But chil-dren of the heavenly King, But children of the heavenly King, May speak their joys a-broad, May speak their joys a-broad.
3. The hill of Zi-on yields A thou-sand sa-cred sweets, Be-fore we reach the heavenly fields, Be-fore we reach the heavenly fields, Or walk the gold-en streets, Or walk the gold-en streets.
4. Then let our songs abound, And ev-ery tear be dry; We're marching thro' Immanuel's ground, We're marching thro' Immanuel's ground, To fair-er worlds on high, To fair-er worlds on high.

Copyright, 1867, by Robert Lowry.

REFRAIN.

We're march-ing to Zi-on, Beau-ti-ful, beauti-ful Zi-on; We're marching upward to Zi-on, The beautiful cit-y of God.

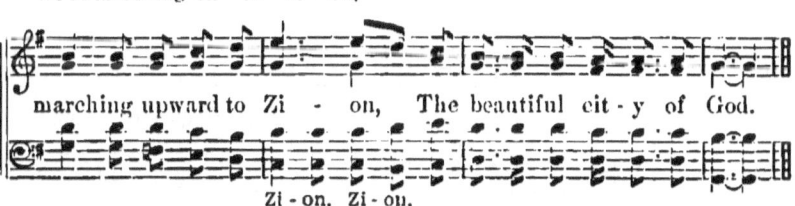

We're marching on to Zi-on, ... thus surround the throne, And thus surround the throne. Zi-on, Zi-on,

No. 200. The Border Land of Canaan.

"They came unto the borders of the land of Canaan."—EXOD. 16: 35.

MYRA JUDSON.   W. H. DOANE.

1. When I sought the ear of the Strong to save, How He
2. On the Bor-der Land there are songs that rise, There are
3. There is more to see, there is more to know, For the
4. When I cross with Him o-ver Jor-dan's tide, And be-

smiled on me and my sins forgave; Now my faith clings fast to my
scenes that burst on my raptured eyes, Till my heart and soul with de-
way grows bright as I on-ward go; There are distant views of the
hold His face on the oth-er side, With a shout of joy I will

Sav-iour's hand, And I walk with Him on the Bor - der Land.
light ex-pand, While I walk with Him on the Bor - der Land.
gold-en strand, That my Sav-iour gives on the Bor - der Land.
bless the hand That was still my Guide on the Bor - der Land.

REFRAIN.

On the Bor - - - der Land of Ca - - naan, On the
On the Bor-der Land of Canaan, hap-py Canaan, bright and fair, On the

Bor - - - der Land of Ca - - naan; Bless-ed
Bor - der Land of Ca-naan, with my Sav-iour walk-ing there; Bless-ed

The Border Land. Concluded.

Bor - - der Land of Ca - naan; Halle-lu-jah, praise the Lord.

Border Land of Canaan, ever happy, bright and fair;

No. 201. Guide Me.

"Lead me and guide me."—Ps. 31: 3.

REV. WILLIAM WILLIAMS.   ROBERT LOWRY, by per.

1. Guide me, O Thou great Je-ho-vah, Pilgrim thro' this bar-ren land;
2. O - pen now the crystal fountain Whence the heal - ing streams do flow;
3. When I tread the verge of Jor-dan, Bid my anx - ious fears sub-side;

I am weak, but Thou art mighty; Hold me with Thy powerful hand:
Let the fi - ery, cloudy pil - lar Lead me all my journey through:
Bear me thro' the swelling current; Land me safe on Canaan's side:

Bread of heaven, Bread of heaven, Feed me till I want no more.
Strong De-liverer, Strong De-liv-'rer, Be Thou still my s'rength and shield.
Songs of prais-es, Songs of prais-es I will ev - er give to Thee.

No. 202. Dennis.

"We have fellowship one with another."—1 John 1: 7.

JOHN FAWCETT, D. D.   H. NAGELI.

1. Blest be the tie that binds Our hearts in Christian love;
   The fel-low-ship of kin-dred minds Is like to that a-bove.
2. Be-fore our Fa-ther's throne We pour our ardent pray'rs;
   Our fears, our hopes, our aims are one, Our comforts and our cares.

3 We share our mutual woes,
  Our mutual burdens bear;
  And often for each other flows
  The sympathizing tear.

4 When we asunder part,
  It gives us inward pain;
  But we shall still be joined in heart,
  And hope to meet again.

No. 203. Guide.

"Who hath also given unto us his holy spirit."—1 Thess. 4: 8.

M. M. WELLS.   M. M. WELLS, by per.

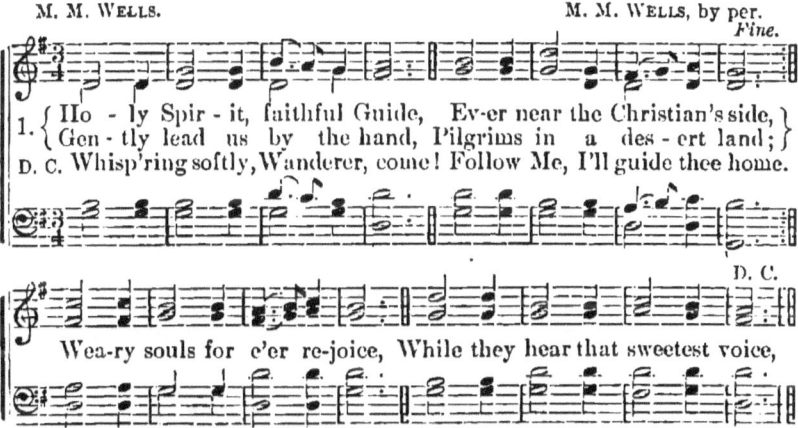

1. { Ho - ly Spir - it, faithful Guide, Ev-er near the Christian's side, }
   { Gen - tly lead us by the hand, Pilgrims in a des - ert land; }
   D. C. Whisp'ring softly, Wanderer, come! Follow Me, I'll guide thee home.

Wea-ry souls for e'er re-joice, While they hear that sweetest voice,

2 Ever present, truest Friend,
  Ever near Thine aid to lend,
  Leave us not to doubt and fear,
  Groping on in darkness drear.
  When the storms are raging sore,
  Hearts grow faint, and hopes give o'er:
  Whisper softly, Wanderer, come!
  Follow Me, I'll guide thee home.

3 When our days of toil shall cease,
  Waiting still for sweet release,
  Nothing left but heaven and prayer,
  Wondering if our names are there;
  Wading deep the dismal flood,
  Pleading naught but Jesus' blood—
  Whisper softly, Wanderer, come!
  Follow Me, I'll guide thee home.

No. 204. Missionary Chant.

"I will proclaim the name of the Lord."—Ex. 33: 19.

B. H. Draper.   H. C. Zeuner.

1. Ye Christian heralds, go, proclaim Salvation in Immanuel's name;
To distant climes the tidings bear, And plant the rose of Sharon there.

2 He'll shield you with a wall of fire,
With holy zeal your hearts inspire;
Bid raging winds their fury cease,
And calm the savage breast to peace.

3 And when our labors all are o'er,
Then shall we meet to part no more;
Meet with the blood-bought throng to fall
And crown the Saviour Lord of all.

No. 205. Sessions.

"And he shall reign forever and ever."—Rev. 11: 15.

Isaac Watts.   L. O. Emerson.

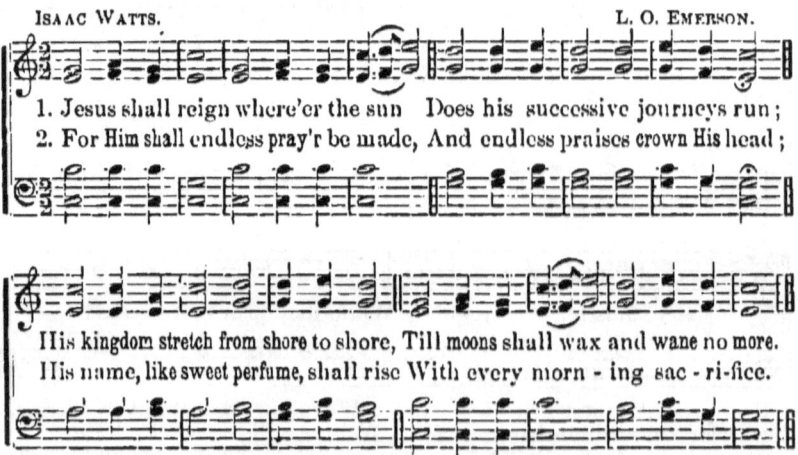

1. Jesus shall reign where'er the sun Does his successive journeys run;
His kingdom stretch from shore to shore, Till moons shall wax and wane no more.

2. For Him shall endless pray'r be made, And endless praises crown His head;
His name, like sweet perfume, shall rise With every morn-ing sac-ri-fice.

3 People and realms of every tongue
Dwell on His love with sweetest song;
And infant voices shall proclaim
Their early blessings on His name.

4 Let every creature rise and bring
Peculiar honors to our King;
Angels descend with songs again,
And earth repeat the loud Amen.

No. 206. Webb.

"The people that walked in darkness have seen a great light." — Isa. 9: 2.

S. F. SMITH. GEORGE JAMES WEBB.

1. The morn-ing light is break-ing; The darkness dis-ap-pears;
The sons of earth are wak-ing To pen-i-ten-tial tears:
D. S. —Of na-tions in com-mo-tion, Prepared for Zi-on's war.
Each breeze that sweeps the o-cean Brings ti-dings from a-far,

2 Rich dews of grace come o'er us,
  In many a gentle shower,
And brighter scenes before us
  Are opening every hour:
Each cry, to heaven going,
  Abundant answers brings,
And heavenly gales are blowing,
  With peace upon their wings.

3 See heathen nations bending
  Before the God we love,
And thousand hearts ascending
  In gratitude above;
While sinners, now confessing,
  The gospel call obey,
And seek the Saviour's blessing—
  A nation in a day.

207 *Our Country's Voice.* 7, 6.

1 Our country's voice is pleading,
  Ye men of God, arise!
His providence is leading,
  The land before you lies:
Day gleams are o'er it brightening,
  And promise clothes the soil;
Wide fields, for harvest whitening,
  Invite the reaper's toil.

2 The love of Christ unfolding,
  Speed on from east to west,
Till all, His cross beholding,
  In Him are fully blest:
Great Author of salvation,
  Haste, haste the glorious day,
When we, a ransomed nation,
  Thy scepter shall obey.
  Mrs. G. W. Anderson.

No. 208. The Highway of the Lord.

"Prepare ye the way of the Lord."—Isa. 40: 3.

Rev. M. Lowrie Hofford.   Robert Lowry.

1. The highway of the Lord prepare, The highway of the King;
2. Let des-ert isles lift up their heads, Let des-ert lands re-joice;
3. The glo-ry of the Prince of Peace Shall cov-er all the earth:
4. The world be-fore Him shall ap-pear, Re-spon-sive to His call;

Let mountains sink, let val-leys rise, And shouts of rapture ring.
Let all the earth in songs of praise U-nite the heart and voice.
And shin-ing wings the ti-dings bear Of our Re-deem-er's birth.
And na-tions bend-ing at His feet Shall crown Him Lord of all.

REFRAIN.

Prepare ye the way of the Lord,   Prepare ye the way of the Lord;
of the Lord,   of the Lord,

Make straight in the desert, make straight in the desert, a highway for our God.

No. 209. Missionary Hymn.

"even all the isles of the heathen."—ZEPH. 2:11.

REGINALD HEBER.   DR. LOWELL MASON.

1. From Greenland's i-cy mountains, From In-dia's cor-al strand,
2. What tho' the spi-cy breez-es Blow soft o'er Cey-lon's isle,
3. Can we, whose souls are lighted By wis-dom from on high,
4. Waft, waft, ye winds, His sto-ry, And you, ye wa-ters, roll,

Where Af-ric's sun-ny fount-ains Roll down their golden sand—
Tho' ev-'ry prospect pleas-es, And on-ly man is vile;
Can we to men be-night-ed The lamp of life de-ny?
Till, like a sea of glo-ry, It spreads from pole to pole;

From many an an-cient riv-er, From many a palmy plain,
In vain, with lav-ish kind-ness, The gifts of God are strown;
Sal-va-tion! oh, sal-va-tion! The joy-ful sound pro-claim,
Till o'er our ransomed nat-ure The Lamb, for sin-ners slain,

They call us to de-liv-er Their land from er-ror's chain.
The heathen, in his blind-ness, Bows down to wood and stone.
Till earth's re-mot-est na-tion Has learned Mes-si-ah's name.
Re-deem-er, King, Cre-a-tor, In bliss re-turns to reign.

No 212. Over the Ocean Wave.

"We should go unto the heathen."—GAL. 2: 9.

MRS. J. W. SAMPSON.   W. B. BRADBURY.

1. O-ver the ocean wave, far, far a-way, There the poor heathen live,
REF.—Pit-y them, pit-y them, Christians at home, Haste with the bread of life,

wait-ing for day; { Groping in ig-norance, dark as the night, }
has-ten and come. { No bless-ed Bi-ble to give them the light; }

2 Here in this happy land we have the light,
Shining from God's own word, free, pure, and bright;
Shall we not send to them Bibles to read,
Teachers, and preachers, and all that they need?

3 Then, while the mission ships glad tidings bring,
List! as that heathen band joyfully sing,
"Over the ocean wave, oh, see them come,
Bringing the bread of life, guiding us home."

No. 213. Benedictus.

"Grace be with you."—2 TIM. 4: 22.

MRS. EDNA L. PARK.   W. H. DOANE.

1. For this sweet hour, O heavenly King, To Thee our thanks, our praise, we bring;
2. And now, dear Saviour, as we part, Impress Thy truth on every heart;
3. Control our thoughts, our foot-steps guide; May peace henceforth in us a-bide;

For this sweet hour, whose light has shone With beams reflected from Thy throne.
And may this precious means of grace Incline us all to seek Thy face.
And may this hap-py service be A day's march nearer, Lord, to Thee.

For closing of service.

No. 216. Rescue the Perishing.

"Lord, save us; we perish."—MATT. 8: 25.

FANNY J. CROSBY.   W. H. DOANE.

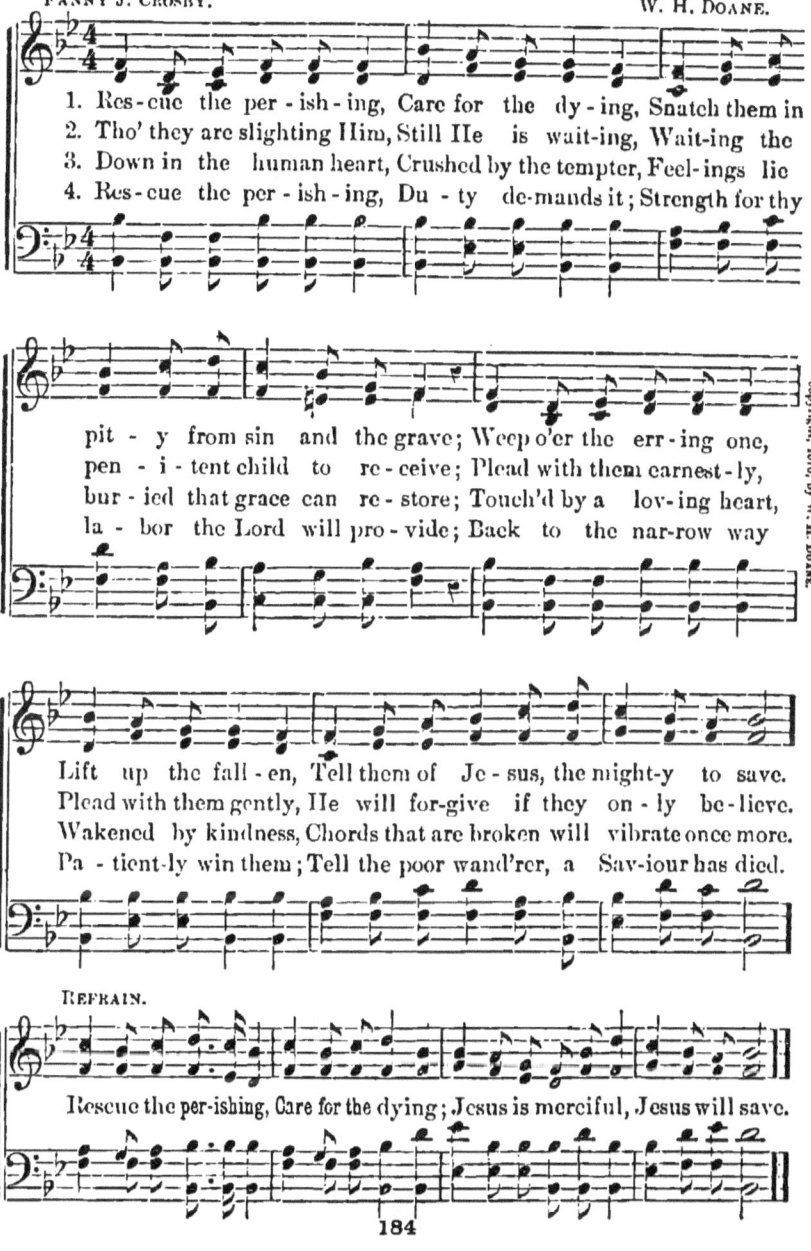

1. Res-cue the per-ish-ing, Care for the dy-ing, Snatch them in pit-y from sin and the grave; Weep o'er the err-ing one, Lift up the fall-en, Tell them of Je-sus, the might-y to save.
2. Tho' they are slighting Him, Still He is wait-ing, Wait-ing the pen-i-tent child to re-ceive; Plead with them earnest-ly, Plead with them gently, He will for-give if they on-ly be-lieve.
3. Down in the human heart, Crushed by the tempter, Feel-ings lie bur-ied that grace can re-store; Touch'd by a lov-ing heart, Wakened by kindness, Chords that are broken will vibrate once more.
4. Res-cue the per-ish-ing, Du-ty de-mands it; Strength for thy la-bor the Lord will pro-vide; Back to the nar-row way Pa-tient-ly win them; Tell the poor wand'rer, a Sav-iour has died.

REFRAIN.

Rescue the per-ishing, Care for the dying; Jesus is merciful, Jesus will save.

Copyright, 1870, by W. H. DOANE.

No. 217. Let There Be Light.

"And there was light." —Gen. 1: 3.

JOHN MARRIOTT. ROBERT LOWRY.

1. Thou, whose al-might-y word Cha - os and dark-ness heard,
   And took their flight, Hear us, we hum-bly pray, And, where the
   Gos-pel day Sheds not its glo-rious ray, Let there be light!

2. Thou, who didst come to bring, On Thy re-deem-ing wing,
   Heal-ing and sight, Health to the sick in mind, Sight to the
   in - ly blind, O now to all man-kind Let there be light!

3. Spir - it of truth and love, Life-giv-ing, ho - ly Dove,
   Speed forth Thy flight; Move on the wa-ters' face, Bear-ing the
   lamp of grace, And, in earth's dark-est place Let there be light!

4. Ho - ly and Bless-ed Three, Glo - ri - ous Trin - i - ty,
   Love, wis-dom, might! Boundless as o - cean's tide Roll-ing in
   full - est pride, O - ver earth, far and wide, Let there be light!

Copyright, 1869, by Robert Lowry.

No. 218. Stockwell.

"Bringing his sheaves with him." —Ps 126: 6.

THOMAS HASTINGS. DARIUS E JONES.

1. He that goeth forth with weeping, Bearing precious seed in love, Never tiring, never sleeping, Findeth mercy from above.

2 Soft descend the dews of heaven,
  Bright the rays celestial shine;
  Precious fruits will thus be given,
  Through an influence all divine.

3 Sow thy seed, be never weary,
  Let no fears thy soul annoy;
  Be the prospect ne'er so dreary,
  Thou shalt reap the fruits of joy.

No. 219. Onward, Christian Soldiers.

"Fight the good fight of faith."—1 Tim. 6:12.

SABINE B. GOULD.   ARTHUR SEYMOUR SULLIVAN.

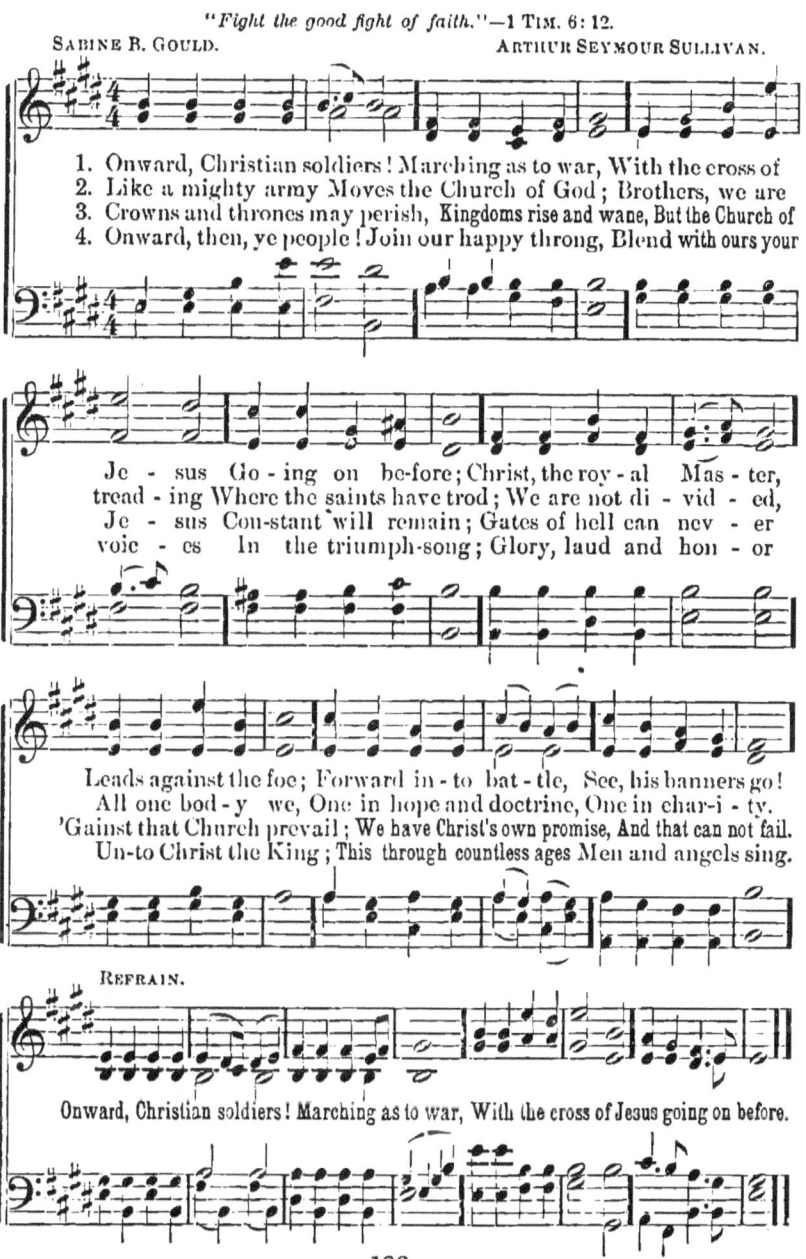

1. Onward, Christian soldiers! Marching as to war, With the cross of
2. Like a mighty army Moves the Church of God; Brothers, we are
3. Crowns and thrones may perish, Kingdoms rise and wane, But the Church of
4. Onward, then, ye people! Join our happy throng, Blend with ours your

Je - sus Go - ing on be-fore; Christ, the roy - al Mas - ter,
tread - ing Where the saints have trod; We are not di - vid - ed,
Je - sus Con-stant will remain; Gates of hell can nev - er
voic - es In the triumph-song; Glory, laud and hon - or

Leads against the foe; Forward in - to bat - tle, See, his banners go!
All one bod - y we, One in hope and doctrine, One in char-i - ty.
'Gainst that Church prevail; We have Christ's own promise, And that can not fail.
Un-to Christ the King; This through countless ages Men and angels sing.

REFRAIN.

Onward, Christian soldiers! Marching as to war, With the cross of Jesus going on before.

No. 220. Go Proclaim the Wondrous Story.

*"Preach the gospel to every creature."—*Mark 16: 15.

Rev. Sidney Dyer.   Robert Lowry.

1. Go proclaim the wondrous sto-ry, Tell how Je-sus loved and died,
2. Dal-ly not in vain de-bat-ing, Men of Is-rael to the strife!
3. Up, ye men of God! nor dal-ly; Con-secrate yourselves to-day;

Till the world, redeem'd, shall glory In a Sav-iour cru-ci-fied;
Hear the cry of mill-ions waiting, Ask-ing for the Bread of Life;
Round the cross of Je-sus ral-ly, He will lead you to the fray;

Bless-ed day! 'tis now be-gin-ning; O-rient beams a-dorn the sky;
Pray and la-bor, bring your treasure, Give yourself, if Je-sus need;
To the bat-tle, brave and steady! "Onward!" be the watchword, "On!"

Glorious triumphs dai-ly win-ning, "Vic-to-ry!" the her-alds cry.
Let it be su-prem-est pleasure Hun-gry souls for Christ to feed.
Crowns and palms for all are read-y, When the fi-nal day is won.

No. 221. Tell it Out.

—"*Tell this, utter it even to the end of the earth.*"—ISA. 48: 20.

FRANCES R. HAVERGAL.   W. H. DOANE.

1. Tell it out among the nations that the Lord is King; Tell it out!
   Tell it out among the nations, bid them shout and sing; Tell it out!
2. Tell it out among the people that the Saviour reigns; Tell it out!
   Tell it out among the heathen, bid them break their chains; Tell it out!

Tell it out! Tell it out with ad-o-ration that He shall increase,
Tell it out! Tell it out among the weeping ones that Jesus lives,
That the mighty King of Glory is the King of Peace; Tell it out with jubilation, let the song ne'er cease! Tell it out! Tell it out!
Tell it out among the weary ones what rest He gives; Tell it out among the sinners that He came to save! Tell it out! Tell it out!

3 Tell it out among the people, Jesus reigns above;
   Tell it out! Tell it out!
Tell it out among the nations that His reign is love;
   Tell it out! Tell it out!
Tell it out among the highways and the lanes at home,
Let it ring across the mountains and the ocean's foam,
That the weary, heavy laden, need no longer roam;
   Tell it out! Tell it out!

No. 222. Arise and Shine.

"Arise, shine; for thy light is come."—Isa. 60: 1.

R. L. ROBERT LOWRY.

1. A-rise and hail the day, Put on thy strength, O Zi-on; Go forth to meet the fray, The bat-tle-hour is come.
2. Fear not to smite the foe, Lift up thy head, O Zi-on; For men and an-gels know The test-ing-time is come.
3. The Lord is on thy side, Rejoice in Him, O Zi-on; Proclaim it far and wide, The triumph-day is come.

REFRAIN.

A-rise, a-rise and shine, Behold, the light is beam-ing; The glo-ry, all di-vine, A-round thy path is streaming; Arise, a-rise and shine For Him whose love has won thee; Behold, the glo-ry of the Lord is ris-en up-on thee.

Copyright, 1889, by Robert Lowry.

No. 223. Light O'er the Hills.

"A light of them which are in darkness."—ROM: 2: 19.

REV. S. F. SMITH. W. H. DOANE.

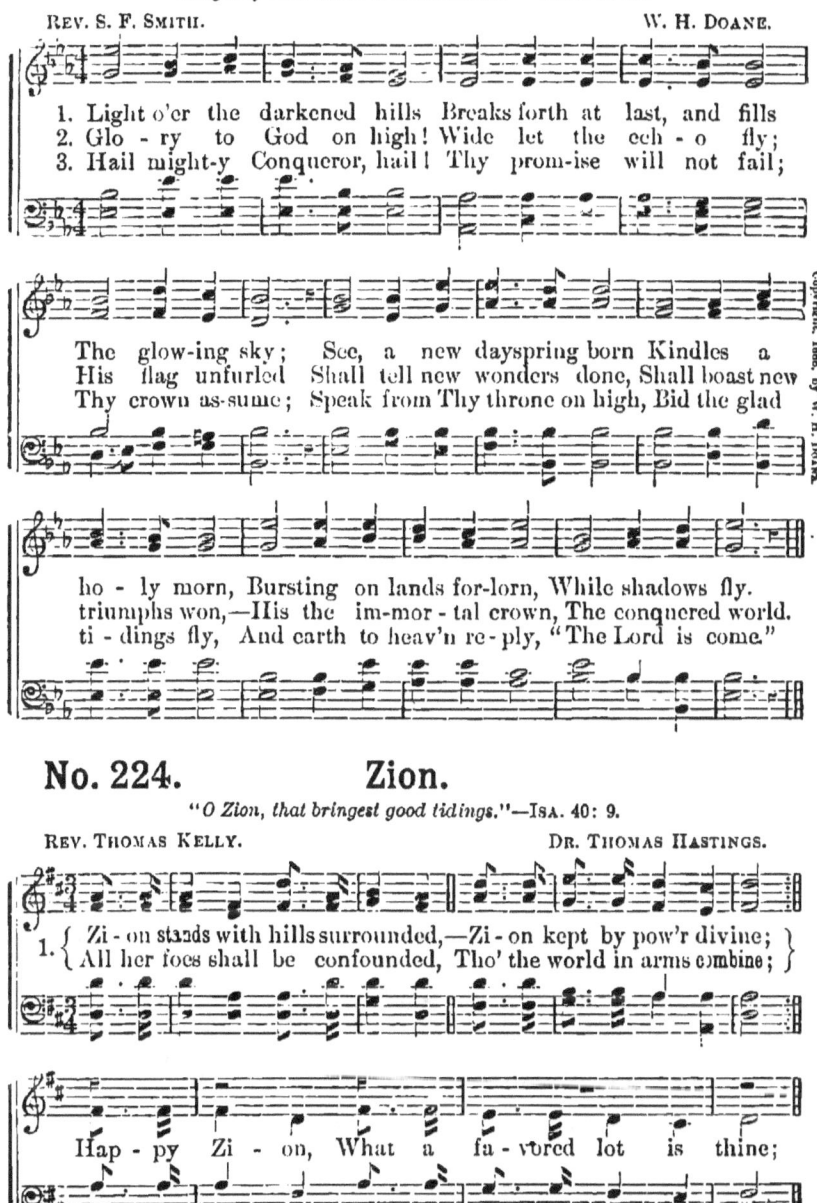

1. Light o'er the darkened hills Breaks forth at last, and fills
2. Glo - ry to God on high! Wide let the ech - o fly;
3. Hail might-y Conqueror, hail! Thy prom-ise will not fail;

The glow-ing sky; See, a new dayspring born Kindles a
His flag unfurled Shall tell new wonders done, Shall boast new
Thy crown as-sume; Speak from Thy throne on high, Bid the glad

ho - ly morn, Bursting on lands for-lorn, While shadows fly.
triumphs won,—His the im-mor - tal crown, The conquered world.
ti - dings fly, And earth to heav'n re - ply, "The Lord is come."

No. 224. Zion.

"O Zion, that bringest good tidings."—ISA. 40: 9.

REV. THOMAS KELLY. DR. THOMAS HASTINGS.

1. { Zi - on stands with hills surrounded,—Zi - on kept by pow'r divine; }
   { All her foes shall be confounded, Tho' the world in arms combine; }

Hap - py Zi - on, What a fa - vored lot is thine;

Zion. Concluded.

Hap - py Zi - on, What a fa - vored lot is thine!

2 God, thy God, will now restore thee;
He himself appears thy Friend;
All thy foes shall flee before thee;
Here their boasts and triumphs end:
Great deliverance
Zion's King will surely send.

3 Enemies no more shall trouble,
All thy wrong shall be redressed;
For thy shame thou shalt have double,
In thy Maker's favor blessed;
All thy conflicts
End in everlasting rest.

No. 225. America.

"The glory of the country." — EZEK. 25: 9.

REV. S. F. SMITH. HENRY CAREY.

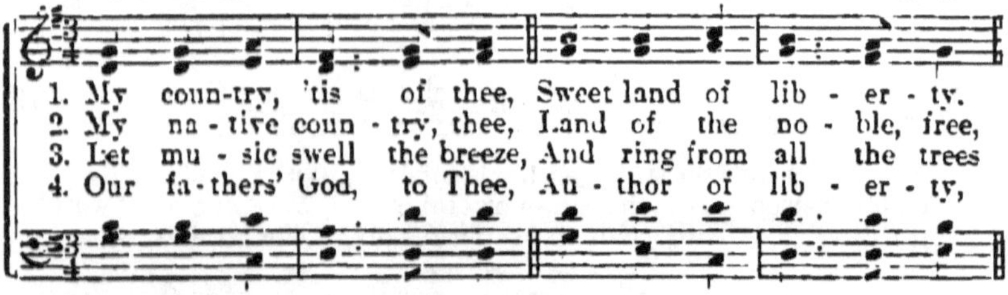

1. My coun-try, 'tis of thee, Sweet land of lib - er - ty.
2. My na - tive coun - try, thee, Land of the no - ble, free,
3. Let mu - sic swell the breeze, And ring from all the trees
4. Our fa - thers' God, to Thee, Au - thor of lib - er - ty,

Of thee I sing; Land where my fa-thers died, Land of the
Thy name I love; I love thy rocks and rills, Thy woods and
Sweet freedom's song; Let mor - tal tongues awake; Let all that
To Thee we sing; Long may our land be bright With freedom's

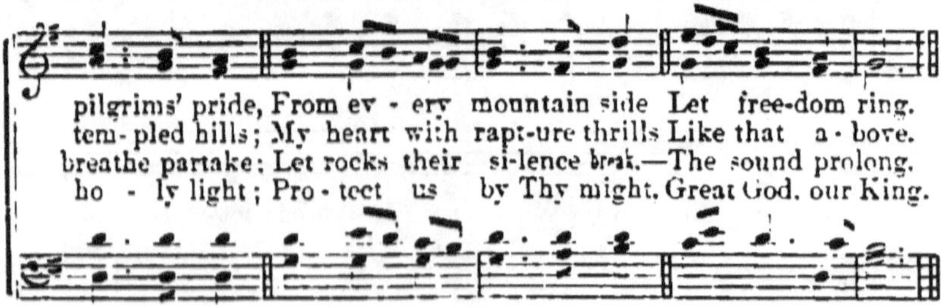

pilgrims' pride, From ev - ery mountain side Let free-dom ring.
tem - pled hills; My heart with rapt-ure thrills Like that a - bove.
breathe partake; Let rocks their si-lence break.—The sound prolong.
ho - ly light; Pro - tect us by Thy might, Great God, our King.

No. 229. Blessed River.

"And he shewed me a pure river of water of life.."—REV. 22: 1.

DR. H. BONAR.   ROBERT LOWRY.

1. Forth from the throne of glo-ry, Bright in its crys-tal gleam,
2. Stream full of life and glad-ness, Spring of all health and peace,
3. Riv-er of God, I greet thee, Not now a-far, but near;

Bursts out the liv-ing fount-ain, Swells on the liv-ing stream;
No harps by thee hang si-lent, Nor hap-py voic-es cease;
My soul to thy still wa-ters Hastes in its thirst-ings here;

Bless-ed Riv-er, Let me ev-er Feast my eyes on thee;
Tranquil Riv-er, Let me ev-er Sit and sing by thee;
Ho-ly Riv-er, Let me ev-er Drink of on-ly thee;

Bless-ed Riv-er, Let me ev-er Feast my eyes on thee.
Tranquil Riv-er, Let me ev-er Sit and sing by thee.
Ho-ly Riv-er, Let me ev-er Drink of on-ly thee.

Copyright, 1871, by Biglow & Main.

No. 230. 'Twill not be Long.

"We are journeying unto the place of which the Lord said, I will give it you."
Num. 10: 29.

FANNY J. CROSBY. W. H. DOANE.

1. 'Twill not be long, our jour-ney here, Each bro-ken sigh and fall-ing tear Will soon be gone, and all will be A cloudless sky, a wave-less sea.
2. 'Twill not be long, the yearn-ing heart May feel its ev-ery hope de-part, And grief be min-gled with its song; We'll meet a-gain, 'twill not be long.
3. Tho' sad we mark the clos-ing eye Of those we loved in days gone by, Yet sweet in death their lat-est song—We'll meet a-gain, 'twill not be long.
4. These checkered wilds, with thorns o'erspread, Thro' which our way so oft is led—This march of time, if faith be strong, Will end in bliss, 'twill not be long.

REFRAIN.

Roll on, dark stream, We dread not thy foam; The pilgrim is longing for home, sweet home.

Roll on, roll on, dark stream, roll on, We

Copyright, 1868, by W. H. Doane.

No. 231. In the Valley.

"They seek a country."—HEB. 11: 11.

MRS. ANNIE S. HAWKS. ROBERT LOWRY.

1. A few more prayers—a few more tears—It won't be long, it won't be long,—A few more months, a few more years, Will hush my song—this earthly song; Then I'll go to my rest, to my rest in the val-ley.
2. A lit-tle pain—a lit-tle joy—And, less or more, it mat-ters not; Some min-gling yet with earth's alloy, And then forgot—ah! soon for-got— While I sleep, calm-ly sleep, calm-ly sleep in the val-ley.
3. A lit-tle gathering of the loved, Whose patient hearts were always true; Some tears to min-gle with the sod—A ver-y few—a ver-y few—When they lay me to rest, me to rest in the val-ley.
4. But Je-sus' love—His precious love, Will be my stay—my on-ly stay; And radiance gleam-ing from a-bove, Will light the way—the lonely way—When my soul pass-es thro', pass-es thro' the dark val-ley.

No. 232. A Few More Partings.

"There remaineth therefore a rest."—HEB. 4: 9.

HORATIUS BONAR. LEONARD MARSHALL.

1. A few more years shall roll, A few more seasons come, And we shall be with those that rest, Asleep within the tomb.

2 A few more struggles here,
A few more partings o'er,
A few more toils, a few more tears,
And we shall weep no more.

3 Then, O my Lord, prepare
My soul for that great day;
O wash me in Thy precious blood,
And take my sins away.

No. 233. Beulah Land.

"The land is as the garden of Eden."—JOEL 2: 3.

EDGAR PAGE.   JOHN R. SWENEY, by per.

1. I've reached the land of corn and wine, With all its rich-es free-ly mine;
2. The Saviour comes and walks with me, And sweet communion here have we;
3. The zephyrs seem to float to me Sweet sounds of heav-en's mel-o-dy,

Here shines undimmed one blissful day, For all my night has passed away.
He gen-tly leads me with His hand, For this is heav-en's bor-der-land.
As an-gels, with the white-robed throng, Join in the sweet redemption song.

REFRAIN.

O Beulah land, sweet Beulah land, As on thy highest mount I stand, I look a-way a-cross the sea, Where mansions are prepared for me, And view the shin-ing glo-ry shore, My heaven, my home for ev-ermore.

No. 234. Numberless as the Sands.

"The number shall be as the sand of the sea."—HOSEA. 1: 10.

F. A. B. Arr.   F. A. BLACKMER. Arr.

Copyright, 1887, by Ira D. Sankey.

1. When we gather at last o-ver Jordan, And the ransomed in glo-ry we see, As the number-less sands of the seashore—What a wonderful sight that will be!
2. When we see all the saved of the ages, Who from sorrow and tri-als are free, Meeting there with a heav-en-ly greeting—What a wonderful sight that will be!
3. When at last we behold our Redeemer, And His glory transcendent we see, While as King of all kingdoms He reigneth—What a wonderful sight that will be!

REFRAIN.

Numberless as the sands of the sea-shore! Numberless as the sands of the shore! of the shore! O, what a sight, 'twill be, When the ran-somed host we see, As numberless as the sands of the sea shore!

No. 235. Oak.

"My rest forever."—Ps. 132: 14

Rev. Thomas R. Taylor.   Dr. Lowell Mason, by per.

1. I'm but a stranger here, Heav'n is my home;
   Earth is a desert drear, Heav'n is my home;
   Danger and sorrow stand
   Round me on every hand; Heav'n is my fatherland—Heav'n is my home.

2 What though the tempest rage,
Heaven is my home;
Short is my pilgrimage,
Heaven is my home;
Time's cold and wint'ry blast
Soon will be overpast;
I shall reach home at last,—
Heaven is my home.

3 There, at my Saviour's side,—
Heaven is my home;
I shall be glorified,—
Heaven is my home;
There are the good and blest,
Those I loved most and best,
And there I, too, shall rest;
Heaven is my home.

No. 236. The Palm of Victory.

"Victory through our Lord Jesus Christ."—1 Cor. 15: 57.

H. C. Page.   Robert Lowry.

1. Aft-er the clouds, the sunbeams Creeping a-cross the lea;
2. Aft-er the toil, the rest-ing; Aft-er the strife, the tomb;
3. Aft-er the wreck, the res-cue; Aft-er the storm, the calm;
4. Then will we sound the pe-an: Where is thy triumph, Grave?

Aft-er the death, the glo-ry God hath ap-point-ed for me.
Aft-er the grief, the gladness—God will dis-pel all the gloom.
Aft-er the bat-tle, vic-tory—God hath pro-vid-ed the palm.
Where is thy sting, De-stroy-er? God hath the pow-er to save.

Copyright, 1869, by Robert Lowry.

No. 240. We Shall Meet.

"*Then shall the righteous shine forth as the sun.*"—MATT. 13: 43.

REV. JOHN ATKINSON.   HUBERT P. MAIN, by per.

1. We shall meet beyond the riv-er, By and by, by and by;
2. We shall strike the harps of glo-ry, By and by, by and by;
3. We shall see and be like Je-sus, By and by, by and by;
4. Wearing robes of snowy whiteness, By and by, by and by;

And the darkness will be o-ver, By and by, by and by;
We shall sing redemption's sto-ry, By and by, by and by;
Who a crown of life will give us, By and by, by and by;
And with crowns of dazzling brightness, By and by, by and by;

With the toilsome journey done, And the glorious bat-tle won,
And the strains for ev-er-more Shall re-sound in sweetness o'er
And the an-gels who ful-fill All the mandates of His will,
Then, our storms and perils passed, And with glo-ry ours at last,

We shall shine forth as the sun, By and by, by and by.
Yon-der ev-er-last-ing shore, By and by, by and by.
Shall at-tend and love us still, By and by, by and by.
We'll pos-sess the kingdom vast, By and by, by and by.

Copyright 1869, by Hubert P. Main.

Some Sweet Day. Concluded.

Some sweet day, We shall meet our loved ones gone, Some sweet day, by and by.

No. 243. Not Now, My Child.

"He .... prayed him that he might be with him."—MARK 5:18.

C. PENNEFATHER. ROBERT LOWRY.

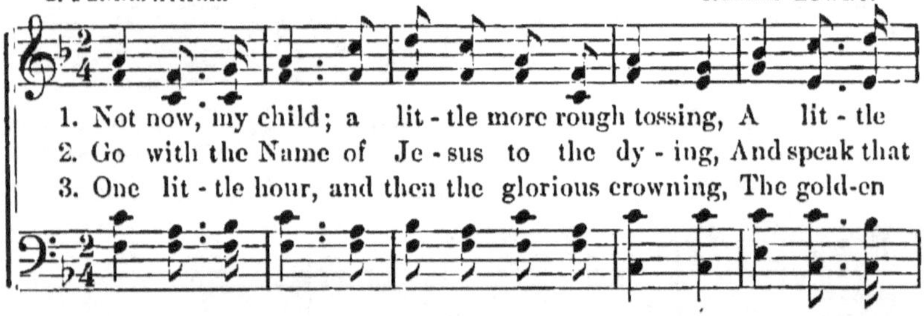

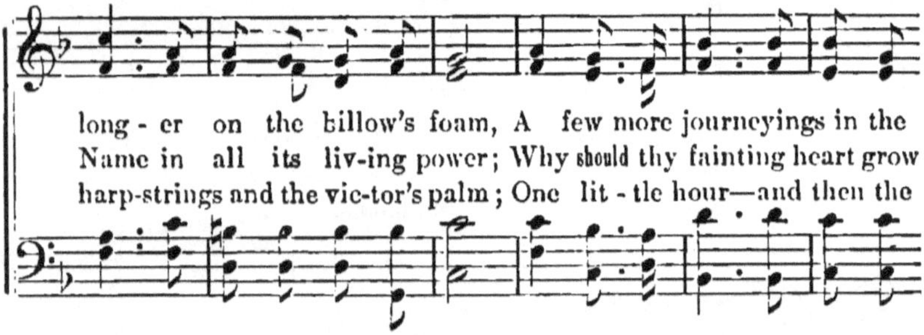

1. Not now, my child; a lit-tle more rough tossing, A lit-tle longer on the billow's foam, A few more journeyings in the des-ert dark-ness, And then—the sunshine of thy Father's home.
2. Go with the Name of Je-sus to the dy-ing, And speak that Name in all its liv-ing power; Why should thy fainting heart grow chill and wea-ry? Canst thou not watch with me one lit-tle hour?
3. One lit-tle hour, and then the glorious crowning, The gold-en harp-strings and the vic-tor's palm; One lit-tle hour—and then the hal-le-lu-jah! All thro' e-ter-ni-ty one grateful psalm.

Copyright, 1868, by ROBERT LOWRY.

No. 244. Home Over There.

"Clothed with white robes, and palms in their hands."—REV. 7:9.

REV. D. W. C. HUNTINGTON.   T. C. O'KANE, by per.

2 O think of the friends over there,
Who before us the journey have trod;
Of the songs that they breathe on the air,
In their home in the palace of God.
Over there, over there,
O think of the friends over there.

3 I'll soon be at home over there,
For the end of my journey I see;
Many dear to my heart, over there,
Are watching and waiting for me.
Over there, over there,
I'll soon be at home over there.

No. 246. Only a Little Way.

"Shortly I must put off this my tabernacle."—2 PET. 1:14.

CORA LINDEN.   W. H. DOANE.

1. 'Tis on-ly a lit-tle way, on to my home, And there in its sunshine for-ev-er I'll roam; While all the day long I journey with song, O beau-ti-ful E-den land, thou art my home.
2. 'Tis on-ly a lit-tle way farther to go, O'er mountain and val-ley where dark wa-ters flow; My Sav-iour is near with blessings to cheer, His love is my guiding star; why should I fear?
3. 'Tis on-ly a lit-tle way; there I shall see The friends that in glo-ry are wait-ing for me; Their voic-es from home now float on the air, They're calling me ten-der-ly, call-ing me there.
4. 'Tis on-ly a lit-tle way o-ver the tide, And there from my Sav-iour no darkness shall hide; The arms of His love will bear me a-long Safe home to the beau-ti-ful E-den of song.

REFRAIN.

'Tis on-ly a lit-tle way, on-ly a lit-tle way, On-ly a lit-tle way on to my home.

Copyright, 1880, by BIGLOW & MAIN.

No. 247. Beyond the Smiling and Weeping.

"There remaineth therefore a rest to the people of God.—Heb. 4 9.

HORATIUS BONAR, D. D.　　　　　　　　　　WM. B. BRADBURY, by per.

1. Beyond the smil-ing and the weep-ing, I shall be soon; Be-yond the wak-ing and the sleeping, Be-yond the sow-ing and the reaping, I shall be soon.
2. Beyond the part-ing and the meet-ing, I shall be soon; Be-yond the farewell and the greeting, Be-yond the pulse's fe-ver beating, I shall be soon. Love, rest and home! Sweet, sweet home!
3. Beyond the frost-chain and the fe-ver, I shall be soon; Be-yond the rock-waste and the riv-er, Be-yond the ev-er and the nev-er, I shall be soon.

O how sweet it will be there to meet The dear ones all at home!

O how sweet it will be there to meet The dear ones all at home!

No. 248. Nearer My Home.

"In my Father's house are many mansions." —JOHN 14: 2.

PHOEBE CARY.   JOHN M. EVANS, by per.

1. One sweet-ly sol-emn thought Comes to me o'er and o'er:
2. Near-er my Fa-ther's house, Where ma-ny mansions be;
3. For e-ven now my feet May stand up-on its brink;

I'm near-er home to-day Than e'er I've been be-fore.
Near-er the great white throne, Near-er the jas-per sea.
I may be near-er home, Near-er than now I think.

REFRAIN.

I'm near-er my home, nearer my home, Nearer my home to-day;

Yes, nearer my home in heav'n to-day, Than ever I've been be-fore.

No. 249. Drawing Nearer.

"A better country, that is, an heavenly."—HEB. 11: 16.

FANNY J. CROSBY.   W. H. DOANE, by per.

1. Drawing nearer my home, drawing nearer to-day, Still my barque hurries on to its harbor a-way, And I smile at the waves while a-round me they roll; There is peace in my heart, there is joy in my soul.
2. Drawing nearer my home, drawing nearer the shore, Where the wiles of the tempt-er will vex me no more; And the light which I now in the distance be-hold, On my vis-ion will break with a splendor untold.
3. Drawing nearer my home, every moment I am, Drawing nearer my home and the throne of the Lamb, Where the ties that were broken a-gain shall u-nite, And our hearts shall be one in e-ter-nal de-light.

REFRAIN.

Drawing near-er home, drawing nearer home, Home, sweet home, home, sweet home.
Drawing nearer my home, drawing nearer my home,

No. 250. By and By.

"The harvest is the end of the world."—Matt. 13: 39.

F. J. C.   Wm. F. Sherwin.

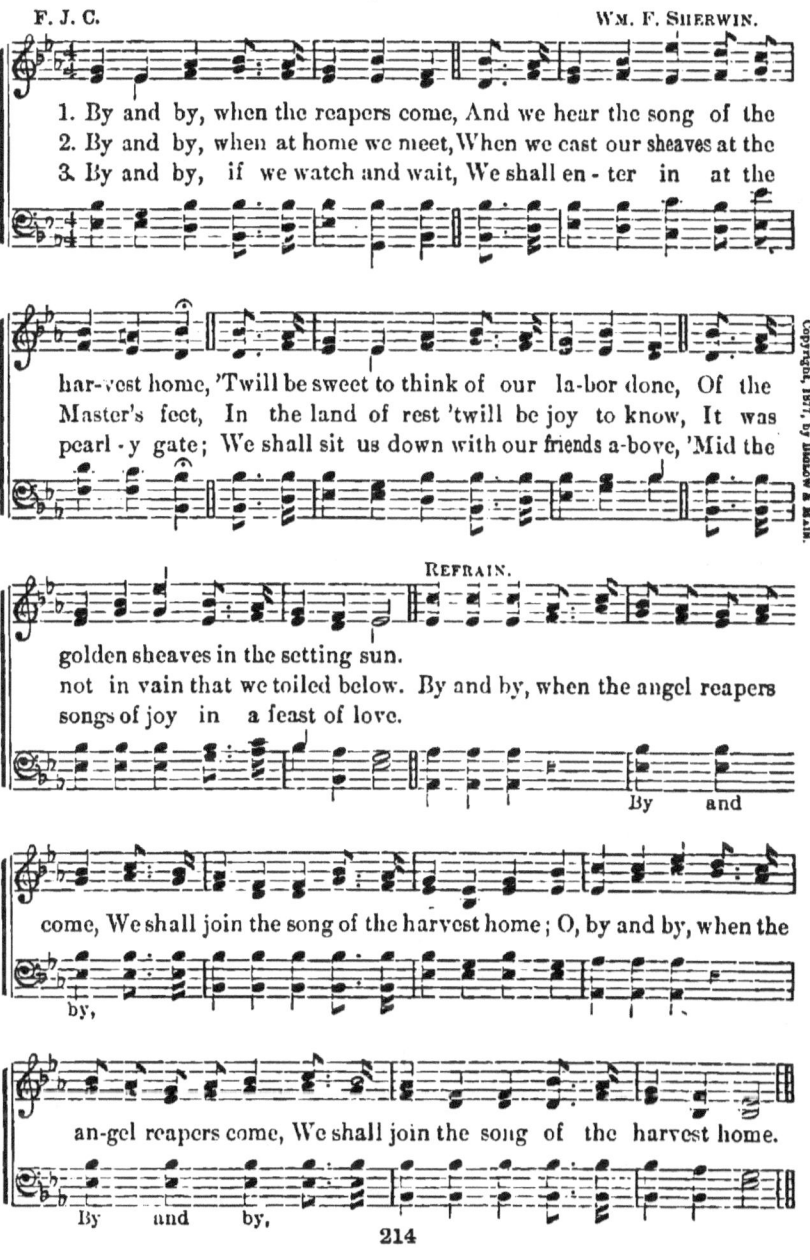

1. By and by, when the reapers come, And we hear the song of the har-vest home, 'Twill be sweet to think of our la-bor done, Of the golden sheaves in the setting sun.
2. By and by, when at home we meet, When we cast our sheaves at the Master's feet, In the land of rest 'twill be joy to know, It was not in vain that we toiled below.
3. By and by, if we watch and wait, We shall en-ter in at the pearl-y gate; We shall sit us down with our friends a-bove, 'Mid the songs of joy in a feast of love.

REFRAIN.

By and by, when the angel reapers come, We shall join the song of the harvest home; O, by and by, when the an-gel reapers come, We shall join the song of the harvest home.

Copyright, 1877, by Biglow & Main.

214

No. 251. Jerusalem the Golden.

"—the holy city, new Jerusalem, coming down from God, out of heaven."—Rev. 21: 2.

BERNHARD, 1140. Tr. Rev. J. M. Neale. ALEXANDER EWING.

1. Je - ru - sa - lem the gold - en, With milk and honey blest,
2. They stand, those halls of Zi - on, All ju - bi - lant with song,
3. There is the throne of Da - vid; And there, from care released,
4. O sweet and bless-ed coun-try, The home of God's e - lect!

Be-neath thy con-tem - pla - tion Sink heart and voice opprest:
And bright with many an an - gel, And all the martyr throng:
The song of them that triumph, The shout of them that feast:
O sweet and bless-ed coun - try That ea-ger hearts ex - pect!

I know not, O, I know not What joys a - wait us there;
The Prince is ev - er in them, The day-light is se - rene;
And they who, with their Leader, Have conquered in the fight,
Je - sus, in mer - cy bring us To that dear land of rest;

What ra-dian-cy of glo - ry, What light beyond com-pare.
The past-ures of the bless-ed Are decked in glorious sheen.
For - ev - er and for - ev - er Are clad in robes of white.
Who art, with God the Fa - ther, And Spir-it, ev - er blest.

SUBJECTS.

The figures refer to the numbers of the hymns.

Activity, 13, 15, 16, 17, 19, 20, 24, 159, 180, 194, 214, 221, 222.
Affliction, 230, 231, 232.
Altogether lovely, 50.
Angels, 127.
As I am, 51, 130, 135.

Battling, 18, 34, 196.
Bearing the Cross, 102, 103.
Beautiful River, 241.
Be not weary, 14.
Be true, 159.
Beulah Land, 233.
Bible, 191, 192.
Blessed River, 229.
Blessing, 10, 69, 70, 85, 89.
Blood of Jesus, 34, 45, 70, 75, 118, 135, 141, 145, 146, 148, 152, 156, 170, 187, 188, 190.
Broken Heart, 39, 153.
By and by, 28, 240, 242, 250.

Christ, coming, 18, 19, 159, 178, 182, 223, 226, 227.
    Crowned, 157, 169, 223, 234.
    Crucified, 54, 168, 171, 187, 189, 190.
    Friend, 45, 46, 58, 74, 75, 91, 112, 154.
    Hiding place, 158.
    Intercessor, 45.
    King, 131, 171, 245.
    Lamb, 65, 86, 116, 134, 135, 138, 142, 146, 148, 189.
    Life, 47, 131.
    Light, 27, 48, 54, 105, 107, 108, 110.
    Love of, 7, 8, 9, 12, 26, 46, 53, 61, 150, 152.
    Reigning, 171, 205.
    Rock, 33, 62, 155, 156, 158.
    Sacrifice of, 45, 175.
    Shepherd, 166.

Closing, 99, 108, 111, 213, 228.
Come now, 136.
Coming to Christ, 82, 89, 95, 118, 120, 130, 135, 139, 141, 153, 156, 176, 179.
Confession, 38, 41, 51, 54, 55, 57, 69, 70, 77, 85, 89.
Consecration, 34, 43, 44, 47, 49, 53, 60, 66, 67, 71, 87, 88, 90, 91, 92, 93, 102, 103, 105, 106, 173.
Coronation, 157.
Cross, 25, 28, 44, 62, 63, 64, 66, 69, 88, 101, 109, 116, 126, 132, 138, 142, 168, 172, 182, 189, 219.

Dependence, 14, 27, 35, 45, 60, 61, 63, 68, 71, 80, 82, 83, 84, 89, 99, 107, 109, 112, 140, 151, 158, 160, 161, 162, 163, 164, 183, 184, 201.
Doubt, 140, 141, 149, 159, 177, 179.
Dying love, 67.

Eden, 237, 246.
Evening, 22, 59, 108, 109.
Even me 121, 144, 175.
Expostulation, 114.

Faith, 43, 49, 54, 57, 65, 66, 68, 79, 93, 100, 105, 113, 132, 140, 141, 154, 161, 162, 163, 164, 165, 172, 184, 185, 195, 197.
Fellowship, 24, 76, 100, 202.
Following Jesus, 43, 105, 129, 200.
Fountain, 11, 31, 124, 142, 152, 201.

Gather them in, 16.
God, communion with, 76.
    Desiring, 85, 86.
    Holy, 3.
    Honor of, 21,
    Infinite, 186.
    Nearer to, 63.
    Our strength, 4, 159.
    Praise to (see *Praise*).
    Promise of, 165.
    Providence of. 195, 201.
    Return to, 123.
    Righteousness of, 215.
    Trust in, 14, 68, 69, 72, 113, 151, 162, 163, 201, 228.
Good old way, 5.
Grace, 100, 111, 112.

SUBJECTS.

Harvest field, 14, 15, 17, 24, 180, 196, 250.
Heaven, 197, 198, 199, 200, 201, 229, 233, 234, 235, 236, 237, 238, 239, 240, 241, 242, 243, 244, 245, 246, 247, 248, 249, 250, 251.
    Home in, 18, 38, 60, 64, 103, 113, 150, 199, 227, 230, 233, 235, 237, 239, 243, 244, 246, 247, 248, 249, 250.

Holy Spirit, 10, 22, 27, 60, 86, 90, 91, 114, 119, 130, 136, 184, 203, 241.
Hope, 5, 14, 33, 197.
Hour of prayer, 30, 72, 76, 81, 82, 98.
House of the Lord, 21.
Humility, 60, 68.
Hunger, 95, 154, 191, 201, 220.

Invitation, 9, 11, 29, 31, 32, 36, 39, 40, 42, 56, 98, 114, 115, 117, 122, 124, 125, 126, 127, 129, 131, 136, 137, 145, 149, 174.
Jesus, calling, 40, 42, 50, 56, 119, 121, 122, 126.
    Indwelling, 48, 60, 90, 91, 99, 105, 106, 173.
    Name of, 116, 167, 169, 170, 171, 205.
    Nearer to, 88, 90, 100, 107, 179.
    Story of, 7, 8, 9, 25, 50, 168.

Joy in believing, 138, 143, 144, 145, 147, 167.

Led, the Christian, 27, 43, 45, 49, 56, 77, 84, 93, 100, 113, 151, 160, 161, 162, 163, 164, 200, 201, 203.
Life and death, 5, 193, 230, 231, 232, 236, 239, 247.
Lily of the Valley, 154.
Love, of Jesus, 7, 8, 9, 12, 26, 46, 53, 58, 67, 75, 97, 103, 155.
    to Jesus, 78, 84, 91, 112.
Loving kindness, 26.

Meet again, 28, 228, 230, 234, 240, 241, 242, 244, 247.
Mercy seat, 6, 36, 67, 73, 76, 85.
Missions, Local, 16, 19, 20, 216, 218.
    Home, 207, 214, 216, 217, 218, 220, 221, 224.
    Foreign, 192, 204, 205, 206, 208, 209, 210, 211, 212, 214, 215, 217, 220, 221, 223, 224.
More love, 12, 44, 53, 78, 91.
Move forward, 15.

National, 207, 225.

Near the Kingdom, 122.
None like Jesus, 79, 132.

Only a step, 125.
Only one foundation, 33, 156.
Only one name, 167.
Only one way, 37, 104.
Only the crumbs, 95.
Open door, 57.
Opening, 21, 30, 50, 85.

Pass me not, 120, 121.
Peace, prayer for, 195.
Pilgrims, 164, 196, 197, 230.
Pilot, 165, 183.
Praise, to Christ, 28, 50, 70, 78, 138, 144, 157, 167, 169, 181, 219.
    to God, 2, 3, 4, 151, 163, 165, 186, 195, 201.
Prayer, 22, 30, 36, 72, 74, 76, 77, 81, 96, 97, 110, 174.
Prodigal, 128.
Promise, 28, 49, 99, 169, 185.

Redeeming work, 134, 143, 148, 166.
Regeneration, 106.
Repentance, 41, 51, 52, 55, 116, 120, 121, 153, 176, 195.
Rescue the perishing, 216.
Rest, 32, 80, 142, 162, 167, 197, 237.
Revival, 2, 10, 22, 23.
Rock of Ages, 62, 155, 156, 158.

Safe in Jesus, 87, 92, 93, 155.
Salvation, 25, 33, 37, 52, 98, 104, 115, 117, 123, 128, 133, 134, 145, 146, 147, 148, 152, 155, 166, 175, 177, 178, 187, 188, 190.
    fullness of, 11, 31, 42, 66, 94, 118, 143, 144, 186.
Second Advent, 226, 227.
Simply trusting, 172.
Sins of scarlet, 123, 178.
Sowing and reaping, 180, 281.

Tell the story, 7, 8, 9, 221.
To-day, 119.
Trinity, 1, 217.

Victory, 34, 37, 133, 185, 196, 236.

Warfare, 13, 159, 182, 219, 220, 222.
White as snow, 89, 118, 123, 143, 173.
Working, 17, 19, 20, 24.
Work, Sing, and Hope, 13.
Worship, 3, 21, 23.

Zion, 198, 199, 222, 224, 251.

217

INDEX.

TITLES AND FIRST LINES.

Titles in SMALL CAPS—first lines in Roman.

	Number.
ABIDE WITH ME	100
Abide with me; fast falls the eventide	100
ABLE TO SAVE	177
A FEW MORE MARCHINGS WEARY	239
A few more marchings weary	239
A FEW MORE PARTINGS	232
A few more prayers—a few more tears	231
A few more years shall roll	232
After the clouds, the sunshine	236
ALAS! AND DID MY SAVIOUR BLEED?	190
Alas! and did my Saviour bleed?	190
ALETTA	117
All hail the power of Jesus' name	157
ALL THE WAY MY SAVIOUR LEADS	161
All the way my Saviour leads me	161
ALTOGETHER LOVELY	50
AMERICA	225
ARISE AND SHINE	222
Arise and hail the day	222
ARISE, O LORD	215
Arise, O Lord, and shine	215
A song, a song of joy	187
At the palace gate confessing	96
AT THY FEET	179
Awake, my soul, in joyful lays	26
BATTLING FOR THE LORD	18
BEAR THE CROSS	103
Bear the cross; the crown will be the brighter	103
BEAUTIFUL RIVER	241
BEAUTIFUL VALLEY OF EDEN	237
Beautiful valley of Eden	237

	Number.
Behold the Lamb of God	146
BE NEAR ME, SAVIOUR	35
Be near me, O my Saviour	35
BENEDICTUS	213
BE NOT WEARY	14
BEULAH LAND	233
BEYOND THE SMILING AND THE WEEPING	247
Beyond the smiling and the weep'g	247
BLESSED HOUR OF PRAYER	30
Blessed Jesus, blessed Jesus	80
Blessed Jesus, God the Lord	179
BLESS ME NOW	69
BLESSED RIVER	229
Blest be the tie that binds	202
BREAD OF LIFE	191
Break Thou the bread of life	191
BRINGING IN THE SHEAVES	180
BRIGHTER, BETTER DAYS ARE COM'G	106
BROKEN HEARTED, EMPTY HANDED	153
Broken hearted, empty handed	153
BY AND BY	250
By and by, when the reapers come	250
By the cross of Christ I linger	168
CAST YOUR CARE ON JESUS	140
Cast your care on Jesus	79
CHILD OF SIN AND SORROW	149
Child of sin and sorrow	149
Children of a King	199
CHRIST RECEIVETH SINFUL MEN	94
CLOSER, CLOSER, LORD, TO THEE	107
Closer, closer, Lord, to Thee	107
Come, burdened souls, with all your guilt	36

TITLES AND FIRST LINES.

Title / First line	Number
COME, COME TO JESUS	137
Come, come to Jesus	137
COME, GREAT DELIVERER	41
Come, O come, with thy broken heart	39
Come, Thou fount of every bless'g	70
Come to the fountain once opened for sin	31
Come with all thy sorrow	32
COME WITH THY BROKEN HEART	39
COME, YE SINNERS	115
Come, ye sinners, poor and needy	115
Come, ye that love the Lord	198
COMING OUT TO MEET US	128
CORONATION	157
Dear Jesus, I long to be perfectly whole	173
DEAR LORD, I NEED THEE	89
Dear Lord, I need Thee all the time	89
Dear Saviour, let Thy watchful eye	60
Dear Saviour, take my hand in Thine	164
DEEPER LOVE FOR THEE	91
DENNIS	202
DEW OF MERCY	97
DISCIPLE	102
Doubt no more thy Saviour's power	177
Down in the valley with my Saviour I would go	43
DRAWING NEARER	240
Drawing nearer my home	249
DRAW ME NEARER	88
DRAW NEAR, O LORD	85
Draw near, O Lord, draw near	85
EVEN ME	121
EVERY DAY AND	84
EVERY DAY W... I BLESS THEE	181
Every day will I bless Thee, each morning and night	181
EXPOSTULATION	114

Title / First line	Number
FATHER, LEAD THOU ME	151
Father, whate'er of earthly bliss	68
FLOWING FOR THEE	124
FOLLOW ON	43
Forth from the throne of glory	229
For this sweet hour, O heavenly King	213
FREELY IT FLOWS	31
From every stormy wind that blows	73
From Greenland's icy mountains	209
GATHER THEM IN	16
Gather them in, for there yet is room	16
GOD BE WITH YOU	228
God be with you till we meet again	228
GOD OF OUR STRENGTH	4
God of our strength, enthron'd above	4
God's tender mercy far exceeds	186
God the all-terrible	195
GO PROCLAIM THE WONDROUS STORY	220
Go proclaim the wondrous story	220
Grant me a deeper love, Saviour divine	44
GRANT US THY BLESSING	23
GRANT US THY PEACE	195
GUIDE	203
GUIDE ME	201
Guide me, O Thou great Jehovah	201
HAPPY DAY	147
HARK! THERE COMES A WHISPER	126
Hark! there comes a whisper stealing on thine ear	126
HASTEN THE JUBILEE	214
Haste thee, pilgrim, on thy journey	196
Heavenly Father, bless me now	69
HE COMES TO SAVE	146
HE LEADETH ME	163
He leadeth me! O blessed thought	163
Helpless I come to Jesus' blood	34
HE PAID THE PRICE	187
Here from the world we turn	22
He that goeth forth with weeping	218
HIDE THOU ME	158

TITLES AND FIRST LINES.

	Number.
His Grace Will Provide	100
Hold Thou Me Up	160
Hold Up the Cross	168
Holy, holy, holy, Lord God Almighty	3
Holy, Holy, Lord	3
Holy Spirit, faithful Guide	203
Home Over There	244
How Much I Owe	193
Humbly Confessing	38
Humbly confessing our need, O Lord, of Thee	38
I Am Praying for You	174
I Am Redeemed	143
I Am Saved	144
I am saved! I am saved!	144
I Am the Lord's, and He is Mine	87
I am the Lord's, and He is mine	87
I am Thine, O Lord, I have heard Thy voice	88
I Am Trusting	66
I am trusting, Lord, in Thee	66
I Could not do Without Thee	45
I could not do without Thee	45
I gave my life for Thee	188
I have a royal message	131
I have a Saviour, He's pleading in glory	174
I Love to Tell the Story	8
I love to tell the story	8
I'm but a stranger here	235
I'm Kneeling at the Door	52
I'm kneeling, Lord, at mercy's gate	52
I Need Thee Every Hour	82
I need Thee every hour	82
In the cross of Christ I glory	101
In the harvest field there is work	17
In the Valley	231
In Thy cleft, O Rock of Ages	158
Is there trouble in your life?	140
"It is finished," Jesus cried	189
I've found a friend in Jesus	154
I've reached the land of corn and wine	233
I Was Glad	21

	Number.
I was glad when they said unto me	21
I Would be a Light	194
I would be a light for Jesus	194
Jerusalem the Golden	251
Jerusalem the golden	251
Jesus Cares for Even Me	175
Jesus, I Love Thee	112
Jesus, I love Thee, Thou art my dearest friend	112
Jesus, I my cross have taken	102
Jesus is Calling	40
Jesus is Here	98
Jesus is tenderly calling thee home	40
Jesus is My Saviour	138
Jesus, keep me near the cross	142
Jesus, Lover of My Soul	61
Jesus, lover of my soul	61
Jesus, my Lord, to Thee I cry	130
Jesus, My Saviour	90
Jesus, my Saviour, cleanse me from sin	90
Jesus Saves!	133
Jesus, Saviour, Pilot Me	183
Jesus, Saviour, pilot me	183
Jesus shall reign where'er the sun	205
Jesus, Thou Lamb of God	116
Jesus Will Help You	42
Just a Little	83
Just a little love, Lord	83
Just as I Am	135
Just as I am, without one plea	135
Just One Way	104
Keep looking up, keep looking up	185
Keep praying as you go	36
Labor On	17
Let my heart be pure from sin	53
Let There Be Light	217
Light O'er the Hills	223
Light o'er the darkened hills	223
Like a Bird to Thee	139
Like the still, gentle fall of the silent dew of night	97

TITLES AND FIRST LINES.

	Number.
Lo! a fountain full and free	11
LONGING FOR CHRIST	176
LOOKING UP	185
LORD, I BELIEVE	141
Lord, I believe; I've heard Thy gracious call	141
Lord, I hear of showers of blessings	121
LORD, IN THY NAME	116
LORD, KEEP ME THINE	105
Lord, my trust I repose on Thee	93
Lord, we beseech Thee, grant us Thy love	10
LOVE OF JESUS	53
LOVING KINDNESS	26
LOWLY AT THY FEET	51
Lowly at Thy feet, O Saviour, I am kneeling	51
Make Thine abode with me	105
Many, many times I have wandered	55
MANY TIMES	55
MARCHING TO ZION	198
MAY THE GRACE	111
May the grace of our Lord Jesus Christ	111
Mine be a hope that is changeless and sure	33
MISSIONARY CHANT	204
MISSIONARY HYMN	209
MORE LIKE JESUS	106
More like Jesus would I be	106
MORE LOVE TO THEE	78
More love to Thee, O Christ	78
MORE, MORE LIKE THEE	44
MOVE FORWARD!	15
Move forward! valiant men and strong	15
MUST JESUS BEAR THE CROSS	64
Must Jesus bear the cross alone	64
My country, 'tis of thee	225
MY FAITH LOOKS UP	65
My faith looks up to Thee	65
MY FAITH STILL CLINGS	54
My heart is a fount'n of joy to-day	143

	Number.
My heart is sad and weary	176
My hope is built on nothing less	156
My sin is great, my strength is weak	54
My soul is happy all day long	133
MY SOUL WILL OVERCOME	34
NAOMI	68
NEARER, MY GOD	63
Nearer, my God, to Thee	63
NEARER MY HOME	248
NEAR THE CROSS	142
NETTLETON	70
NO NAME SO SWEET	171
NONE LIKE JESUS	79
NO ONE KNOWS BUT JESUS	58
No one knows but Jesus How sinful I have been	58
NOTHING BUT THE BLOOD	118
NOT NOW, MY CHILD	243
Not now, my child: a little more rough tossing	243
Now crucified with Christ I am	47
NUMBERLESS AS THE SAND	234
OAK	235
O CHILD OF GOD, BE TRUE	159
O child of God, be true	159
O come to the fountain of mercy and love	124
O FOR A CLOSER WALK	86
O for a closer walk with God	86
O happy day that fixed my choice	147
O hear my cry, be gracious now to	41
O LET ME TELL IT ONCE AGAIN	9
O let me tell it once again	9
O let us live nearer to Jesus our Lord	100
O LIGHT OF LIGHT, SHINE IN	48
O Light of light, shine in	48
O my Saviour, may Thy Spirit	148
ONE BLESSED HOUR	81
One blessed hour with Jesus our Lord	81
ONE MORE DAY OF TOILING	24
One more day of toiling	24

TITLES AND FIRST LINES.

Title / First Line	Number
One sweetly solemn thought	248
One there is above all others	75
ONE TRUE WAY	37
ONLY A LITTLE WAY	246
ONLY A STEP TO JESUS	125
Only a step to Jesus! Then why not take it now?	125
ONLY ONE FOUNDATION	33
ONLY ONE NAME	167
ONLY THE CRUMBS	95
ONLY THE LOVE OF JESUS	12
ONWARD, CHRISTIAN SOLDIERS	219
Onward, christian soldiers	219
O Saviour mine, who now beholdest me	160
O Saviour, we pray Thee, send out Thy sweet light	210
O the blessed cross of Christ my story	25
O think of a home over there	244
O THOU LAMB OF CALVARY	189
O THOU THAT HEAREST PRAYER	110
O Thou that hearest prayer	110
O TO BE OVER YONDER!	238
O to be over yonder!	238
O to think the Lord of glory	175
O turn ye, O turn ye, for why will ye die	114
OUR COUNTRY'S VOICE	207
Our country's voice is pleading	207
OVERFLOWING EVER	11
Over my spirit, silently musing	166
OVER THE OCEAN WAVE	212
Over the ocean wave, far, far away	212
PASS ME NOT	120
Pass me not, O gentle Saviour	120
PATH OF LOVE	184
PRAISE YE THE FATHER	1
Praise ye the Father, for His loving kindness	1
PRECIOUS NAME	169
PRECIOUS PROMISE	165
Precious promise God hath given	165
Precious Saviour, dearest Friend	91
RATHBUN	101
REACH ME THY HAND	56
Reach me Thy hand, my child	56
REDEEMING WORK	134
Redeeming work is done	134
RESCUE THE PERISHING	216
Rescue the perishing, care for the dying	216
REST IN JESUS	32
REST IN THEE	80
RETREAT	73
ROCK OF AGES	62
Rock of Ages, cleft for me	62
SAFE IN THE ARMS OF JESUS	155
Safe in the arms of Jesus	155
SAVED BY THE BLOOD	148
Saviour, behold in Thy mercy now	95
SAVIOUR, DEAR SAVIOUR	46
Saviour, dear Saviour, More than all the world beside	46
Saviour, grant us now Thy bless'g	23
SAVIOUR, KEEP ME	71
Saviour, keep me ever Thine	71
Saviour, like a bird to Thee	139
SAVIOUR, LISTEN TO OUR PRAYER	77
Saviour, listen to our prayer	77
Saviour, more than life to me	84
SAVIOUR, TAKE MY HAND	164
Saviour, the day is declining	59
Saviour, Thy dying love	67
SAVIOUR, TO THY MERCY SEAT	6
Saviour, to Thy mercy seat	6
SESSIONS	205
Shall we gather at the river	241
SHOWERS OF BLESSING	10
Simply trusting all the way	172
Sings my happy soul of Jesus	178
SINKING OUT OF SELF	47
Sinners Jesus will receive	94
SINS OF SCARLET	173
SOLID ROCK	156
SOME SWEET DAY, BY AND BY	242
SOMETHING FOR JESUS	67
So near to the Kingdom	123

TITLES AND FIRST LINES.

	Number.
So near to the Kingdom! yet what dost thou lack?	122
Sowing in the morning, sowing seeds of kindness	180
Spread, O spread, thou mighty word	192
STOCKWELL	218
SWEET HOUR OF PRAYER	72
Sweet hour of prayer, sweet hour of prayer	72
SWEET MOMENTS OF PRAYER	22
SUN OF MY SOUL	108
Sun of my soul, thou Saviour dear	108
TAKE ME AS I AM	130
Take the name of Jesus with you	169
TAKE THE PROMISE	99
Take the promise as you go	99
Take the wings of the morning	29
TALMAR	75
TELL IT OUT	221
Tell it out among the heathen that the Lord is King	221
TELL IT WITH JOY	145
Tell it with joy, tell it with joy	145
Tell me the old, old story	7
THE BANNER OF THE CROSS	182
THE BLESSED CROSS, MY STORY	25
THE BORDER LAND OF CANAAN	200
The glad, glad news that Jesus came	214
THE GOOD OLD WAY	5
THE HALF CAN NEVER BE TOLD	186
THE HIGHWAY OF THE LORD	208
The highway of the Lord prepare	208
THE HUMBLE HEART	60
THE ISLANDS ARE WAIT'G FOR THEE	210
THE KING IN HIS BEAUTY	245
THE LILY OF THE VALLEY	154
THE LORD IS MY LIGHT	27
The Lord is my light, then why should I fear?	27
THE MERCY SEAT	76
THE MISTAKES OF MY LIFE	57
The mistakes of my life are many	57

	Number.
The morning light is breaking	206
THE NAME I LOVE	170
THE OLD, OLD STORY	7
THE PALACE GATE OF PRAYER	96
THE PALM OF VICTORY	236
THERE ARE ANGELS HOVERING	127
There are angels hovering round	127
THERE IS A FOUNTAIN	152
There is a fount'n filled with blood	152
There is a name I love to hear	170
There is but one true way	37
There is just one way for us all to come	104
There is no name so sweet on earth	171
There is only one Name that the saints adore	167
There's a royal banner given for display	182
THE ROYAL MESSAGE	131
The Saviour is calling you, sinner	42
The whole wide world for Jesus	211
THE WIDE WORLD FOR JESUS	211
Thine, most gracious Lord	92
THIS I DID FOR THEE	188
THIS I KNOW	93
Thou gracious Lord, enthroned above	76
THOU HAST REDEEMED ME	166
Thou, whose almighty word	217
THOUGH YOUR SINS BE AS SCARLET	123
Tho' your sins be as scarlet	123
'Tis only a little way, on to my home	246
'Tis the blessed hour of prayer	30
TO-DAY THE SAVIOUR CALLS	119
To-day the Saviour calls; Ye wanderers, come	119
TO THE WORK	19
To the work! to the work! we are servants of God	19
To work for Jesus and His cause	13
TRUSTING JESUS	172
TRUST IN GOD, MY BROTHER	113
Trust in God, my brother, All the days to come	113

TITLES AND FIRST LINES.

Title / First Line	Number
'TWILL NOT BE LONG	230
'Twill not be long, our journey here	230
Vesper bells are ringing	50
We are children of a King	199
We are going forth with our staff in hand	5
WE ARE PILGRIMS OF A DAY	197
We are pilgrims of a day	197
WEBB	206
Weeping soul, no longer mourn	117
WEEPING WILL NOT SAVE ME	132
Weeping will not save me	132
WE GLORY IN THE CROSS	28
We glory in the cross, Praise the Lord	28
We have heard the joyful sound	133
WE PRAISE THEE, O GOD	2
We praise Thee, O God, for the Son of Thy love	2
We're saved by the blood	148
WE SHALL MEET	240
We shall meet beyond the river	240
We shall reach the summer land	242
We shall see Him in the better land	245
We stand on holy ground	98
We've listed in a holy war	18
WHAT A FRIEND IN JESUS	74
What a friend we have in Jesus	74
What can fill my soul with joy?	12
What can wash away my stain?	118
WHAT IS ALL THE WORLD TO ME?	49
What is all the world to me?	49
When I sought the ear of the Strong to save	200
When Jesus comes to reward His servants	227
WHEN THE BRIDEGROOM COMETH	226
When the bridegroom cometh	226
When the clouds are gathering round thee	14
When this passing world is done	193
When we gather at last	234
When we turn to God and leave the path of sin	128
Whether the journey be short or long	151
WHISPER A MESSAGE	59
WHITER THAN SNOW	173
WHO'LL BE THE NEXT?	129
Who'll be the next to follow Jesus	129
WHOLLY THINE	92
WHY DO YOU WAIT?	136
Why do you wait, dear brother?	136
WILL JESUS FIND US WATCHING	227
WINGS OF THE MORNING	29
WITH GENTLE HAND	162
With gentle hand He leadeth me	162
WONDERFUL LOVE	150
Wonderful love that found us	150
WORD DIVINE	192
WORK, FOR THE NIGHT	20
Work, for the night is coming	20
WORK, SING AND HOPE	13
Ye christian heralds, go, proclaim	204
ZION	224
Zion stands with hills surrounded	224

www.ingramcontent.com/pod-product-compliance
Lightning Source LLC
Chambersburg PA
CBHW022014220426
43663CB00007B/1081